Rose's War

By Rose Boy

Rose's War
(Formally The 10th Mountain in Me)

In honor of my WWII 10th Mountain Division father.

Table of Contents

Chapter One
A Cradle in the Vieux Carre

"Ma'am, you're under arrest. Your zipper must be on the side or in the back of your pants," said the police officer. It was the mid-fifties. By the age of seventeen the girl that would eventually be my mother was coming out into the world. Ellie and her girlfriends lived in New Orleans on the Eastbank of the mighty Mississippi River. On weekends they would cross the river to the Westbank to dance and party at a dance hall on Fourth Street in Westwego, which was southwest of New Orleans. It was "Laissez les bon temps rouler" which meant, "Let the Good Times Roll." It wasn't long before Ellie laid eyes on the man of her dreams. She assured her girlfriends that she was going to marry him. I'm sure they had a good laugh. It was too soon for Ellie to know there would be an obstacle and a force to be reckoned with which was Toby's mother, Agnes. Toby lived several miles south of Westwego, which was not a Main Street town; it was more like a village off the highway. It was on the way to the small town of Lafitte, a fishing community on Bayou Barataria.

The laugh was on Ellie's girlfriends. After a few dances, a short courtship, and before the happy couple was eighteen, they were talking about getting married; however, talking is all they did. Toby once stood on a bridge and threatened to jump if he couldn't marry Ellie. His mother was not going to approve of a marriage between the two of them. Soon after this, they didn't need her approval anymore, and they tied the knot eagerly. I'm sure they were anticipating living life "happily ever after."

Ellie defied her mother-in-law, and it didn't make Agnes like her one iota more. She still had a problem with the lady closest to her beloved. Perhaps it didn't happen overnight, but at some point Toby started going to his mother's house after he got off work to eat supper. When he finally arrived at his own house, Ellie would be humiliated. By the time he walked in the door, the only thing flaming was Ellie. She had supper waiting, but had to eat alone. Perhaps he thought her cooking was not palatable, but Ellie didn't care what he thought. She was not about to play second fiddle to her mother-in-law.

Pregnant with her first child after having been married almost two years, she decided to abandon her marriage. She became a wild child at twenty years old and moved to the French Quarter in New Orleans, where she rented her own apartment. At this point, her baby boy was born. Without an education, Ellie's job options were limited, so she chose to work as a bartender in different bars in the French Quarter. She didn't have a car and didn't need one; she could walk to work. She wasn't concerned about the things one would worry about if one had a car, such as the cost of a car, gas, tires, and any other incidentals having to do with a vehicle. Her expenses were baby related, and a babysitter was mandatory.

A week before Easter, Ellie's baby boy, named after his father, was approximately eight months old. The baby had not laid his little eyes on his father, nor had Toby met his son. At this particular time her babysitters were two lesbian girls. After work, as usual, Ellie rushed home to her baby boy, but the baby was gone, never to be seen again. Ellie alleged the babysitters ran off with Toby, Jr. There was an investigation, but it didn't bring the baby home. To this day Ellie has never heard anything about her firstborn. Many years later her husband told me that he and his mother always believed that Ellie sold the baby. Personally, I don't really know which side of the story to believe. I can't find any reason to believe my mother but every reason not to believe her.

I was not yet a gleam in Ellie's eyes, but within a year of her baby's disappearance, she started having an affair with a man twice her age. He would frequent the bar where she worked for a beer or two. Obviously, they had taken the relationship to another level. She found out that she was pregnant with me at twenty-one years old. Although the new man in her life was the father, this is not the story Ellie would tell.

Ellie was sitting on the stoop in front of her apartment building. The stoop was a flat area at the bottom of the steps where you could actually sit. It probably was an area designed to place a potted plant or a small tree. She was celebrating her duck in the oven and wearing her first maternity top when, out of the blue, she spotted Toby strutting towards her. She dashed upstairs to change into a regular blouse. Toby ended up spending the night on her sofa. He wanted to let her know that he had been drafted and would be leaving soon. She couldn't care less because her mother-in-law made it impossible for her to live with him.

I was born Christmas Eve, 1955, at 9:05 am at the notorious Charity Hospital. Two weeks later, I was baptized at Saint Louis Cathedral. The church is graced by the back of Jackson Square and is located a couple of blocks from the Mississippi River.

Since she was still married and was not going to get divorced, she decided she was going to live this lie – a lie about which I would neither know nor understand for thirty-three years. It didn't stop her from claiming her estranged husband was my father. Not long after I was born, she was entitled to receive approximately thirty-five dollars in monthly assistance from the government because her husband was enlisted.

We lived in the 900 Block of Esplanade Avenue and ratted around the French Quarter on foot when I reached the age of two. We would walk several blocks out of the French Quarter across Canal Street to Rampart Street to buy my dresses from the Cinderella Store.

Perhaps it was while living in the French Quarter in my first years of life – with all of the colorful flowers and the scent of sweet olive blossoms drifting down any street at certain times of the year – that my affinity for color and floral fragrances began.

My mother would take me with her to visit her bartender friend at the famous Lafitte's Blacksmith Shop Bar on the corner of Bourbon and St. Philip Street, located in the heart of the French Quarter. His name was probably just Al, but my mother called him Ally-oop. Maybe it was a name she'd heard in a song, or maybe it was a pet name. Lafitte's Blacksmith Shop Bar is supposedly the oldest bar in the United States. It is named after Jean Lafitte, who was a notorious pirate and an integral part in the Battle of New Orleans in 1812.

As much as I'd like to remember the time from birth to three years old, I don't have much recollection. Maybe it's because I constantly had a different babysitter, since my mother worked all of the time and I rarely got to see her, other than on her two days off from work every week. Eventually, my mother's mother came to stay with us. My mother said they would laugh at me because I would hide my grandmother's shoes to prevent her from leaving.

My grandmother's bloodline consisted of Irish and Spanish in addition to an Indian tribe from the Mississippi area. She was very lean, with a head of thin, short gray hair. I remember thinking that her eyes were very different, or maybe I had never seen eyes with that placement.

It didn't bother me that she drank and was drunk most of the time. She would let me sit on the kitchen floor and pull all of the pots and pans out of the cabinets to entertain myself. Even though I don't remember a lot about that time frame, I have that picture etched in my brain. The pots were both my musical instruments and my mother's cooking utensils. She mostly fed me Campbell's Pork-n-Beans out of little cans, so the pots were rarely used anyway. After a short period of time, Grandma, for whatever reason, departed, and I became a one-man band.

By the time I was a little over a year old, my mother was pregnant again and having the second baby allegedly by her gentleman friend. The baby was born at the beginning of December, and this led to the commencement of another lie. When she brought him home from the hospital, I was waiting at the far end of the hall with my arms extended toward her, and I wanted to see my baby brother, Andrew. I actually named him. My mother couldn't figure out how I came up with that name. The name my mother had picked out for her new baby boy would then become his middle name.

Unfortunately, Andrew was born with asthma, and my mother made a decision to adopt him out to an older couple related to one of her best friends. They lived in the country about one hundred twenty miles west of New Orleans. This was an area just outside the city limits of Jeanerette, a little Main Street town on Bayou Teche between Morgan City and New Iberia. They didn't have any children together, however, there was a much older daughter from his adopted mother's previous marriage. They would be able to afford the medical attention Andrew needed and would love him as their own.

Of course I don't remember, but my mother told me there was a very popular toy for little girls at the time. It was a red wooden-handle broom. It was a replica of a regular household broom, but a miniature at about three-feet long. We walked to the nearest grocery store. As we passed the toy section, I saw the broom and started screaming because I wanted it, but my mother would not buy it for me. She said I had one at home. As we checked out at the register, I was still having a temper tantrum. We exited the store. When we got to the corner, I was still screaming and squirming in her arms. I then fell out of her arms unto the sidewalk. She quickly took me to the hospital, where the doctor said I would be fine.

It's pretty much unheard of and difficult to believe, but my mother claims she was constantly arrested for wearing pants with a zipper in the front. A police officer would pull up on the side of her as she walked down a street in the French Quarter. The officer would get out of his car, approach her, and ask her to lift her blouse so that he could see if she had a zipper in the front of her pants. After being arrested numerous times, my mother decided to rent an apartment that was located within walking distance to the jail. Obviously, she was determined to wear what she wanted.

I'm not sure where, why, or how she got it, but my mother ended up with a relative's government check in her pocket. When she was arrested for the last time, the police found the check that would begin her troubles. She was charged with a federal offense and would serve a ten-month sentence in a federal prison in West Virginia. At an early age my mother was "a ward of the state." She didn't want the same thing to happen to me. She appointed Agnes to be my caretaker for ten months. Her arrangements consisted of her showing up at Agnes's house, telling her about the situation, and handing her a bag of clothes and, of course, me.

Most kids beam and gleam when they talk about their grandmothers or grandparents, but it's not like that for me. I don't get those warm, fuzzy feelings. My maternal grandmother couldn't be bothered with assuming the responsibility for her granddaughter while her daughter was incarcerated, and the godmother my mother chose didn't step up to her role either.

Can you imagine having to leave your baby? Can you imagine being the baby left behind? I was too young to know, but someone should have told me, "You'll be living with a lady who hates your mother, but, not to worry, she might like you." What was my mother thinking, or was she? I had never met my paternal grandmother, and I was terrified from the beginning because they were fussing, fighting, and arguing with fingers pointing and hands flying in the air. As my mother departed, they were screaming at the top of their lungs. I was only three years old and didn't have a clue of their previous relationship.

Agnes already had it figured out and knew I was not her son's daughter, however, he was married to my mother, and his name was on my birth certificate, so no one else questioned the paternity.

I was not blind. Even at three years old, I could see the hate for me in my grandmother's eyes. Agnes had a couple of sons that still lived at home. Her second husband, Ralph, had a big presence, probably because of his loud voice, but I didn't fear him. I suppose his loudness aided him in his position as a game warden, a job that required him to be bullish. I remember being very fond of him. Maybe he could feel my fear, and his heart went out to me. Most of the time, he had a smell of Vick's Vapor Rub about him. I was constantly looking out of the front door for my mother to return, but all I ever saw was a 1950 F1 Ford panel truck which belonged to her oldest son. It wasn't long before that, that she found a new home for me.

Agnes had a niece Lavon who lived a couple

of miles further down the road. This was Lavon's second marriage. Travis was thirty-four years old and Lavon was thirty-nine. She was the daughter of one of Agnes's brothers. A few years earlier Lavon had been married for the first time, had a hysterectomy, and was told by the doctor that she would not be able to conceive. She begged her husband for the available baby girl. And so it was a done deal. I was delivered to their doorsteps. Lavon and her husband Travis were going to be my new momma and daddy.

Lavon was a homemaker and Travis a public school bus driver just like his father-in-law. Lavon's parents were called Maw and Paw. Paw had retired, and Daddy inherited his position and the school bus. My new momma was probably thrilled, because until then her husband worked offshore, and she was probably a little lonesome as a newlywed, especially since she was very self-centered. Even as a grown-up, she was spoiled rotten by her parents.

Momma's parents lived next door to us. They were, for some reason, the foster parents to their adopted son's first baby boy, Putsy. Maybe it was because Putsy's parents were only fourteen and fifteen years old and maybe because his mother was pregnant again. It didn't take his parents long to have a grand total of five kids. Putsy was only a year younger than I, and Lavon already had been getting attached to Putsy for two years before I arrived.

I was so sad and cried a lot because I missed my real mother so much. Upon arrival at my new foster home, I slept in a baby bed. Every morning I woke up and urinated on myself. One morning Momma and Daddy waited for me to do my thing and spanked me right on the spot. For years they would brag I never did that again. Now, looking back, it seems like I was their experimental toy. Once again, it was not about me. I vividly remember rocking myself to sleep on my knees in a fetal position, butt up in the air. Maybe that was my comfort zone, back to the womb. For some weird reason at three years old, I guess I knew not to confront my new parents about my yearning for my real mother. I cried in private.

The living room was at the front of the house. From this room there was access to the screened porch, which led outside the house. This area was just steps away from the highway. That entrance was rarely, if ever, used. I remember Momma and Daddy talking about how they awoke one morning to find me walking out of the porch's front door. They considered it sleep walking. Could I possibly have simply been trying to leave in order to find my real mother? A few months before I arrived, a toilet was installed in their bathroom with the bathtub. Prior to this, there had been an outhouse towards the back of the property, which was not acceptable for Momma.

I was in a new place with many things to explore. My curiosity was constantly working overtime, and I was into anything I could see and everything I could get my hands on. First, it was the little aluminum Sucrets throat lozenges can full of straight pins. In my mouth they went. Momma would spot it from across the room. Of course she was screaming while making a mad dash to come to my rescue to get the pins out of my mouth.

The next week it was the container of marbles. In my mouth they went, and Momma screamed and came running once again. One night Momma went to play bingo. As my explorations continued, I was digging in Momma's dresser drawers. This particular night I hit the jackpot. I found her spare lipstick. I'm sure I must have been fascinated with the red lipstick she wore. I loved anything that was colorful. I was attempting to put the lipstick on my lips, but it ended up all over my face, hands, and down the front of my pajamas. About that time Momma came home and saw my face and thought it was blood. Of course, she screamed and was relieved when she realized it was lipstick and not blood as she had suspected.

If I'd had more toys, I probably would not have been so exploratory. One of my first inexpensive toys was a hard plastic lady bug that had a string that when pulled caused it to climb up the refrigerator door. While watching it climb it's way to the top of the refrigerator, it lost suction and ended up smacking me in the nose. My nose began to bleed. Not only did I cry, but it was also traumatic being attacked by a toy. That was the end of the fascination. Putsy's toys (which kept us entertained for some time) were three-or-four-inch-high green plastic cowboy figurines and brown Indians as well. There was war between the cowboys and Indians on a daily basis.

My first holiday with my new family was Easter, and it was great. I had been with them for three months. I got a huge straw Easter basket. It must have been two and a half feet wide and four inches deep with a handle. I had never seen anything so magnificent. It was very colorful, and I can still remember being thrilled. It had a stuffed bunny rabbit, chocolate bunnies, jelly beans, plastic eggs, miniature malted Easter eggs, and orange sponge slices sprinkled with sugar and nestled in plastic, shiny green moss. The basket was filled with goodies, and I was filled with joy. The basket was larger than I was.

It was at this point Momma advised Daddy that if he couldn't also buy one for the baby Putsy, he was not to buy one for me. It was probably becoming very clear to Daddy at this point that sibling rivalry was in full force. Putsy and I were not siblings, but there was rivalry around every corner.

Daddy was not easily excited; however, one day he was looking for me, and I was nowhere to be found. With no luck he repeatedly searched our small house from one end to the other; he began to panic. As a last resort he went to our neighbors, but they had not seen me either. One of the ladies came to our house, and she found me behind the big rocking chair, playing with my paper dolls.

At three years old I don't think I was intentionally ignoring my daddy's call to me. I was simply in my own little corner of the world with my paper dolls.

My first Christmas with my new Momma and Daddy gave them the biggest thrill. We got dressed up to go see Santa at Maison Blanche on Canal Street. Of course, we had a photo taken. I would carry that photo with me the rest of my life. I loved Mr. Bingle, the snowman, and looked forward to our reunion as well. He was the cutest little furry white snowman and was ornate with a colorful scarf and bells attached that jingled. This was my second Christmas on Santa's lap; I was getting accustomed to that red and furry man's lap. Momma and Daddy said I told Santa I wanted a "wocking" chair and some peanuts. They never could figure out where I came up with that notion.

Daddy's relatives lived in west Texas. His mom and stepdad lived in Big Spring. Daddy's two sisters and three brothers – each with a spouse and a child or two – lived within a hundred miles or so. Until this time Daddy didn't have much in common with his siblings, and they didn't like the idea that he left Texas to live on the bayous in Louisiana. Since I completed their family, we would take a vacation to West Texas every summer because they now had something in common and fit in perfectly.

Next door, Maw and Paw bought a gym set with a slide, a double swing, and a seesaw for Putsy. Since I lived next door, I had access. The swing set was extremely welcome. While Putsy and I were playing on the set, he put his finger between the bars and smashed his thumb. He went inside crying, and I got fussed at and whipped. It was definitely my fault. His thumb and fingernail were mutilated, and that was the only scar he'd have for a lifetime.

Momma was a seamstress and enjoyed sewing matching dresses for us. The drug store where Momma got her prescriptions filled had a lunch counter. She bragged that when we ate there, everyone at the counter commented on how precious I was, so well mannered and well behaved. Most of all, they commented on how beautiful my dress was. I know she enjoyed me at first. Things couldn't have been any better. Children added dimension to everything in her life, and now she had her very own little girl.

When I was four years old, Momma and

Daddy decided I should be taking dance lessons. They got in touch with that witch-of-a-grandmother of mine. They wanted her to ask Toby if he would let them adopt me. He didn't want to have anything to do with me, his answer was no. Life went on without official papers.

Looking back at the old dance review photos, it was obvious how different I was compared to the other little girls who were actually born on the Bayou. They all had olive skin, dark hair, and dark eyes. I had auburn hair, a fair complexion, and hazel eyes. I was Cajun as a pecan. Momma would make my costumes. The mothers of the other little girls would hire Momma to make their daughters' costumes as well. Momma enjoyed working night after night gluing sequins and sewing with the satin and tulle. She enjoyed all the fussing about how beautiful the costumes were, not to mention she got paid for doing something she loved and enjoyed.

Momma and Daddy joined a bowling league and would leave me next door with Maw, Paw, and Putsy on the nights they bowled. We played, but we fought even more. Maw would stand in the middle of us, and we would go round and round in circles around her, swinging and trying to hit each other. Every once in a while we would accidentally smack Maw. Sometimes I wanted to hurt Putsy.

One time I watched him running towards me and saw my opportunity to crush his pride or at least see him cry a bit. I sat down and stuck my leg out to trip him. It was a perfect plan, since he went flying horizontally down the hall. It was rare that I could get him back for always being the pet. It was worth the fussing I got. Sometimes Paw would be fussing at both of us, and we would look at each other and die laughing. That would make Paw even madder.

The month before my fourth birthday, my mother was released from prison. Ellie went to her mother-in-law's home only to find me not there. Someone told her where I was. She didn't have a clue that she was about to lose custody of me forever. She came to the house where I was, but Momma and Daddy were not about to let her take me. The old grandfather came out with a shotgun and told her to get the hell off his property. Actually, it was my parents' property, but she got the message. Daddy went next door to get the constable, Mr. Steve. He came over and told my mother not to come back without a court order. I was in bed sick with measles, but I could hear the commotion. Although my mother was not timid, she was unsuccessful in this case.

A few weeks later I thought my wishes and prayers to God were coming true. My mother was back with a court order for visitation for my birthday. She also had that man that I remembered always visiting us before she went to jail. He just sat there. Neither he nor I said a word. It was 1959 and the new life-size doll Patti Play Pal had made her debut. They were thirty-five dollars, and my mother was proud to bring one to me. Probably because I had reddish hair, I had the one with red hair. My new parents wouldn't let me keep it; they said it was too big. My mother's gentleman friend said he was going to the car to get the Chihuahua puppy he had brought for me. He was quickly informed that it wouldn't be necessary because I couldn't have a dog. My mother and her friend were gone before I knew it.

I had never heard of or knew about Toby, especially as a biological father. So with two mommies, finally a daddy, and people saying I looked just like my new hazel-eyed foster daddy, I was finally either figuring out my roots or getting more lost in my head. I didn't give one thought to how unusual it was that I had ended up in Travis and Lavon's family, because it felt like home. But, I had the most difficult time trying to understand the change of family members. I wasn't told I would have to forget all the previous people and names in my life.

Approximately two weeks later my mother returned with another court order for a visitation for the entire weekend. I can remember us backing out the driveway and pulling away in her car. I also remember standing on her front passenger seat, holding my round, clear, hard acrylic purse that Momma had given me. I don't know if I inherited the purse, or if she bought it for me. I was a happy camper. By the end of our visit, my mother was not about to return me because I was telling her about the whippings I had gotten because of Putsy.

At some point during our visitation, I asked my mother, "Why do I have to have two mommies?" My mother mustered up an answer and said, "God thought you needed a lot of people to love you." Fifty years later that simple question and answer would still bring a stream of tears to my eyes and make my heart ache.

My mother had her mother take me to the place where my brother was living with his adopted family. It didn't take long for the Sheriff's Office to locate me and haul me down to the jail house where my foster momma and daddy picked me up. I remember watching them walk up the corridor towards me and feeling happy to see them. I was back to my familiar surroundings.

I was back home and enjoying the bathtub, but I didn't enjoy the way Momma shoved the corner of the face towel up one nostril at a time. I had never experienced such a brutal act. It was something I could have lived without. One night Momma came in and screamed differently than she had in the past. Before I knew it Daddy and Momma were in the bathroom with me, laughing hysterically. I had a turd floating to the side of me in the bathtub. Other than my picture being taken with Santa Claus, pictures were a rare occurrence, but they thought this scene warranted a photo.

It was my second Christmas in my new home. All I wanted for Christmas were my two front teeth. For the life of me, I cannot figure out how Daddy got away with building a beautiful play house for me as my big Christmas present. It was huge – eight by ten feet – and larger than our bathroom. I fell in love with it. It was a typical miniature Acadian house – white with pink trim on the door and window frames. It even had a front porch with two steps. Momma made curtains that matched. The floor was linoleum. There were little, green aluminum appliances; a little, brown wooden dinette table; and two chairs. I loved the ironing board and plastic iron. There was a wisteria vine near the window, which provided me with a constant air freshener during spring.

I am not sure if they thought Putsy would have tea with me in my playhouse, but it didn't happen. I would cry in there and pray to God to bring my mother back to me again. We went to church every Sunday. We also had a Bible at home (which I don't remember opening), but that didn't stop me from praying a lot. That was the extent of my knowledge of God.

One day it started to rain really hard, but it was not lightening. Trapped in my playhouse, I could see the chickens standing in the rain and was so upset, because I wanted them to come inside with me. I couldn't understand why they would want to stay in the rain when they could have come in my house. I called over and over for them, but they never came in. There was a very mean black rooster that chased me one time, pecked me on the butt, and made me bleed. Although I didn't hold a grudge and desperately wanted anyone's company, I still wasn't about to invite him in.

One time while Momma was at the back door talking to me in the yard and I was nonchalantly circling my playhouse, hanging onto and dragging my hands across the window sill, my finger suddenly swiped a caterpillar. That simple conversation turned into a screaming episode in a moment's time. I scared the daylights out of my momma. She came running and realized what had happened. By this time, screaming was a part of our everyday life and not uncommon.

Daddy would go next door to help Mr. Steve put toys together for his boys. I don't remember the boy's toys but was told they were "gas stations." They were old-fashioned ones, with toy cars that could be pushed in the garage area. Lucy's mom would fix hot cocoa for them. Daddy probably would have preferred a hot toddy.

Graf's Half Way House was across the highway from the neighborhood restaurant down the street from our house. It was a very long, narrow, and small-hole-in-the-wall known as the neighborhood bar. Daddy would also frequent this place for a beer and to buy cigarettes. He and Momma had just purchased a used light-yellow convertible Studebaker that looked great and had very little mileage. Daddy was only going to be there a few minutes but became distracted long enough for me to find a hammer on the floorboard. I started pounding on the windshield. Daddy didn't know what I was capable of, and before long he was quickly returning to the car because he had been informed by a friend who had witnessed the incident.

Momma and Daddy's property was about one-fifth of an acre. There was a ditch that lined one perimeter. Daddy had placed a board that was wide enough to serve as a bridge to get to a wooded area on the other side. We used to cross over to pick blackberries when they were hanging from the vines. One day Putsy was crossing and fell into the approximately three-foot-deep water. The good news was that it was summer, so the water was not cold. When he popped up and was pulled out by an adult, there were a couple of crawfish latched onto his toes. I couldn't help but laugh on the inside while he was screaming bloody murder on the outside.

Every once in a while my wicked grandmother would come over to our house. I could still see the devil in her eyes. It was even more obvious she hated me, and she was not making me crazy about her, either. I wished I would never have to see her again. I was always afraid she would take me back. I didn't realize that was the last thing on her mind. She didn't come over very much, and I now realize that she probably had her own fears where I was concerned. I had begun to get more adjusted to my new family and was feeling comfortable with having consistent faces around me.

On many occasions as we drove home from a night of my parents' playing cards at a relative's house, Momma had a few too many drinks and, as usual, was an out-of-control, screaming maniac. Their arguments were extreme and scary. I always had a fear that our family would be destroyed and fall apart. They were still arguing as we walked up the driveway from the car to the house. Momma tugged at Daddy's arm. Just wanting to get her off his arm, he lightly pushed her and she fell. Of course it was Daddy's fault. She screamed, "I hate you," and a little later I said, "Daddy, I still love you." I think it melted his heart.

New relatives constantly visited us or Maw and Paw's next door. They were very warm, friendly, and loving people. Paw was totally bald and shiny on top. He had a couple of front teeth missing, a bit of a pot belly, and always wore khaki pants with a little cuff. He was physically handicapped from birth, with one leg missing at the knee and one hand with only three fingers.

Paw sported a wooden leg during the course of the day and had an old homemade wooden crutch for times when his wooden leg was off. The crutch was actually carved from a tree trunk. After he had retired from driving the school bus, he scrapped metals. It looked like he worked really hard. We could hear him banging on the metals for hours at a time. Paw was also very political and was always involved in campaigning for his political friends. Maw and Paw were nice to me, but I could feel and see their favoritism for Putsy; however, this didn't bother me. Maw still had the compassion to comfort me sometimes when I needed it. The only thing that separated the two houses was a driveway. Even though it was next door, it felt like a haven away from home.

Occasionally, Paw would take us with him to deliver fish to the fish market in the French Quarter. It seemed like a real hustle and bustle. Paw would go every week. There was no air conditioning in the vehicles, so the ice that surrounded the fish in the bed of the truck soothed the air. It smelled of fresh seafood, the food of the sea. I really enjoyed the times I went with him.

Paw used to tell us stories from his past. During the depression, when the bayous were the highways, they traveled in their pirogues (canoe-like boats) and eventually crossed the river to New Orleans. He talked about how they trapped beavers for their pelts. He used to pick moss from the trees, which was cured and made into mattress stuffing. They would get twenty-five cents for a truckload. Could that have been top pay for that time period? I wanted to know if he picked more than one load a day. He couldn't remember, and I would think I could never forget something like that.

It was at one of those campaign parties that I first heard of a king-size bed. Several of the children, including myself, were jumping up and down on the mattress until we were red in the face. It was like we were in another world, because none of the adults ever came to stop us. It was so much fun that I could have stayed there all night jumping.

My daddy was a very likable guy also. Everyone enjoyed being at our house or rather in our yard. Daddy was in heaven when he had a crab, shrimp, or crawfish boil or a barbecue. He knew all the kids and teenagers in the area because he drove the school bus. For Mardi Gras, Daddy invited everyone to load up the bus with relatives and their children. We parked the bus on St. Charles Avenue and camped out the entire day.

My old dance-review costumes still fit, and they played an important role for dressing up for Mardi Gras. Daddy put me on his shoulders so I could scream and catch beads and trinkets. In the late fifties the Mardi Gras beads were glass and could be dangerous, if not deadly. Daddy never complained about the injuries he sustained from them pounding his face and forehead. Putsy and I took turns being on Daddy's shoulders. He didn't even complain about his neck being red and raw from my tutu.

Occasionally, I would get to ride with Daddy on his evening bus route. His bus was one of seven for the West Jefferson High School in Harvey or "Upfront". Harvey was about ten miles north of where we lived. While he was waiting for school to let out, one of the other drivers would sit in his bus, and they would shoot the breeze while waiting for school to be dismissed. I was diligently watching this bus driver while he was pulling some tobacco out of the cellophane pouch. My eyes were following his every move. Daddy saw my interest, so he asked me if I wanted to try some. Of course I said "yes" and was dipping my little fingers in the pouch when Daddy slapped it out of my hand before I had the chance to put it in my mouth.

A similar event (and the next explosive adventure) came not long after this. Daddy was sitting on our sofa in the living room smoking a cigarette. I was watching him and thinking I might want to try smoking. It looked like a lot of fun. Daddy could see my interest peaking and gave me a cigarette. I took a little puff and Daddy said you need to bring it down deeper into your belly. I did and

I went flying into the bathroom to throw up in the toilet bowl. At the ripe age of four and a half, I suppose he thought the best way to teach me right from wrong was the hard way. Perhaps this was my clue that life would be a constant challenge.

Our third trip to west Texas was definitely a "Cajun Vacation." Daddy invited another family of relatives consisting of Aunt Marney, Uncle Burke, two daughters, and a son. We loaded up the bus. It was definitely more fun to have some company of kids closer to my own age. On the way home we stopped to dig up cactus to bring back to Louisiana. Their middle daughter ended up falling into a bunch of cacti. When they turned her over, we could see the splinters all over one eye. I wanted to scream. We rushed to find the nearest hospital, where the doctor removed the splinters and cleaned the area. Soon after this, we were on our way back home.

Seemingly, because of all the excitement or because I was squirming and could not sit still, Momma hit me on the head with a comb while combing my hair. I was about to make the biggest mistake of my little life by turning around and spitting at her. I had never spit before and do not know what possessed me to do it. Of course I shocked everyone. She disciplined me, but I didn't realize she would hate me for the rest of my life. I'm sure that was the first and last time I would spit ever. Thus my "Paved Road to Hell" began. She never let me forget the mistake I'd made. From that day on she began beating me for any reason.

Chapter Two
My New School Bag

I started school just before I was five years old because my birth date was at the end of December. At the end of my first day of school when Daddy came home from his bus route, he brought home a surprise for me. He told me to go in the school bus, and I would find it. I was very surprised because it wasn't Christmas or my birthday. I couldn't believe my eyes. I was already really liking school. The surprise was my very first schoolbag. I was overjoyed. It was green, white, red, and black plaid, like that of a kilt skirt. It had black vinyl on the inside. I had never seen anything so shiny except for my black patent-leather shoes. On the front there were two buckles to fasten it closed, and there was an adjustable shoulder strap. I was very proud and happy to go to school sporting my new schoolbag. It was a pivotal moment for me.

Daddy bragged all the time because I already knew how to spell my name before I started school. I was becoming Daddy's little girl. I followed him like a shadow and couldn't wait for him to come home in the evenings.

In the first year Momma would have to get up to get me off to school. If I left the cap off the toothpaste, she would whip me. When I left the towel in the wrong place, she would whip me. Sometimes, if I was moving too slowly, she'd whip me. Momma would make me wear my school dress two consecutive days. I didn't have a problem with that, and I'm not sure if anyone else noticed or cared. I remember her complaining about having to starch my dresses. It seemed like she was always ironing my dresses.

I always told Daddy that Momma whipped me all the time. I guess I thought if I told Daddy, he would make it stop, but it didn't stop. She would find places on my body that were not visible. She would pull my hair, put her hand over my mouth so I couldn't breathe, or just get really close to my face. The look on her face and the screaming really intimidated and terrified me. Was it possible that the loss of Momma's baby from years before magnified her anger towards me?

First grade was the best and the easiest, and I loved my teacher, Mrs. Moore. She had black hair that was very wavy, fluffy, and out of control. Her lips were a little wrinkled, and she wore red lipstick. She had poor posture and was somewhat hunched over. She probably looked older than she really was. She was very thin, almost skinny, but very sweet and soft spoken and a little less than patient after a point.

I think Mrs. Moore liked me, but she didn't like me having to go to the bathroom as much as I did. One time she said I could not go to the restroom, and I urinated on myself. She brought me to the bathroom and washed my undies. We went back into the classroom, and she hung my underwear on the heating pipes that were near the ceiling at the back corner of the room. At five years old it didn't matter; however, several years later I would realize how some third or fourth grade boys never forget. They can be very cruel. They coined the word "Stinky" for me. I can't say that didn't bother me.

When Putsy and I got home from school, Maw started having a treat of French bread and butter with coffee diluted with boiled cream and sugar.

Maw had a little brown bottle, like the bottles of vanilla extract, but this one was root beer extract to which she added water and sugar. Perhaps a couple of times a month, Maw would make homemade root beer for us. The only soda I knew about were the little bottles of Coca Cola, so I welcomed the delicious change.

It was the first time I'd ever seen little foiled paper stars, and there was glue on the backside to attach it to your assignments. Perhaps they were red, green, blue, and gold and were awarded according to the grade on the assignments. They didn't have a star for talking, so I never was awarded any.

One evening after school while waiting for my bus, I was crying under a tree. A much older girl named Roxsanna came over and asked why I was crying? I told her, "Because no one will listen to me." She said, "I'll listen to you." I'm not certain, but I probably told her this lady is not my mother and when I get home, she is going to beat me because my button was missing, my hem was ripped, or I had a stain from lunch. Roxsanna had the face of an angel and reminded me a lot of my real mother. I'm not sure if the resemblance was due to the way she spoke, the way she looked, or her demeanor.

Momma and Maw mostly spoke in French to each other. I could speak a little, but I understood more. Momma had several choice French names for me when she was angry, which was often. She would say I was just like my mother, and I didn't know what that meant, but it was hurtful never-the-less.

It seemed like I was always crying when I left for school and crying when I came home. There were never any bruises, but the beatings were not imaginary. I always thought of the girl under the tree as my angel. She would share her Mallo Cup candy bar while we waited for our buses, and it did make me feel better, even if it was just for the moment. I was devastated because she went on to junior high school, and I never saw her again.

Evidently, I had a big problem. A few times my teacher made me wear an "I am a busy body" sign on my back hanging down by a string around my neck. At five years old I didn't care; I didn't recognize embarrassment. I had much more than a sign to worry about at the end of the day.

It was about this time I met Lucy, Mr. Steve's daughter. She was a year older than I.

Momma and Daddy started playing friendly card games with Mr. Steve and his wife Ms. Camille. On the weekends after supper we would go to their house for hours while our parents played pinochle. Lucy and I would play in her room. She had lots of toys and things to play with. One night after our parents finished playing cards, Daddy came in to wake me up to go home. Before we fell asleep, we tied our legs together with a fluorescent lime-green plastic jump rope. When Daddy pulled the sheets down and saw how we had tied ourselves together, he had to go get the other adults. Their laughing woke us up.

Lucy had a single bed with a button-tufted, blonde leather headboard, cushioned perfectly for what we wanted to do. We would try to balance each other on our hands, knees, and feet. While one was lying down, the other was getting slammed into the headboard, the wall, or the floor. We played and laughed for hours, enjoying every moment. I loved playing with Lucy. Her mother had a really unusual and funny laugh, which I could listen to all day. It was like a cackle. It was nice not to hear any fussing or have glaring ugly eyes intimidating me.

I think it was the way Momma took care of me when I was sick in bed with measles, a cold, a problem with my tonsils, or the flu (which happened at least twice a year, mostly during the winter) which drew me to her. I loved her, even though she beat me. After she'd whip me and I began to cry, she'd cry, hug me, and say she was sorry and that she loved me. I would then say I was sorry, but for what, I never knew.

Lucy had five older brothers. One got married and moved out, and she inherited his phonograph and forty-five vinyl records. We loved to dance. The one song that I remember was "Seven Little Girls" (Sitting in the Backseat with Fred) sung by Paul Evans and The Curls. Freddy was also her second-oldest brother's name. We would open her bedroom window so we could hear the music in the yard, where we danced barefoot in the grass. We were so curious about kissing. We would kiss our arms, our clothes, the tree, and the walls. That's what the song was about, kissing in the backseat with Fred. Once we tried to kiss each other, exploded with laughter, and ended up spraying each other with our saliva. Our lips never actually touched, but our stomachs ached from laughing so much.

I was not at Lucy's house when her mother got the phone call that her oldest son had been killed in a car accident, but the next day it was obvious something terrible had happened. Her family was devastated, and her mother was distraught.

Not long after, her mom perhaps wanted a distraction and bought a snow cone machine. There was a table in the back corner of their garage and the machine was sitting on that table. The machine crushed the ice cubes. My life was changing for the better at this time. My biggest problem was deciding if I wanted grape, spearmint, or strawberry. Snow cones were at the top of my favorite list. I was only allowed to get one every two weeks if I was lucky. I asked my daddy how I could get more snow cones. He said I needed to make some money.

I was only five years old when one of Daddy's sister's family came to visit for the first time. We had to drive across the very narrow Huey P. Long Bridge to cross the river to pick them up from the New Orleans Airport. On the way back I was looking out of the car window at the ground far below. I thought the real cars were miniature toy cars. Aunt

Gail bought a match box car for me before she left to return home.

I would get a lucky break when another one of Daddy's sisters, her husband, and their son and daughter started visiting us from west Texas. I was thrilled because I would get extra snow cones. The niece and nephew were funny as could be. The girl was on crutches, and based on the way they fought and argued, it was not surprising. To say the least, I was amused. I didn't want them to leave, and looked forward to their next visit. They were a little older than I, and it amazed me that they spoke Horse Latin. I couldn't believe they could speak this language. I insisted on them proving it to me, which they did.

They left and my money-making plan was set in motion. The magnolia tree in the front yard would play a huge role in my path to colorful lips, depending on what flavor I chose. I would sit on a small homemade wooden bench made for one person. I would sell pecans, pears, or figs — whatever was blooming at the time.

One day I was at Lucy's house. Perhaps her mom was sleeping. I 'm sure she thought that the little girls could do no harm. We were about six years old. We found some scissors and had a great idea. We were going to trim each other's bangs. She did okay on the first half of mine but put a big gash on the other half. I was just about to return the favor when her mother came in and saved the day for Lucy. I'm the one that ended up getting the grief. Her mother simply told her she's not supposed to be cutting anyone's hair. Needless to say, my next school picture showed evidence of that episode.

In between Lucy's and our house was a nice lady who had a much older daughter. She and her husband were separating. I didn't quite understand this because her husband was there a lot. I had never heard of divorce. I didn't realize that he still had a daughter that he had to visit. That lady's best girlfriend often visited her and they would play cards for nickels and pennies. They allowed me to come over and hang around the table while Momma was sleeping. If they dropped any coins on the floor, they let me keep the ones I found. They probably could hear Momma screaming and fussing at me and could see I had been crying most of the time. I didn't realize the pity but sure did appreciate the coins. I guess everyone felt sorry for me.

They would also send me to the restaurant for a package of Pall Mall cigarettes. I would put the quarter and the nickel in the cigarette machine, and I got to keep the four pennies that were attached to the side of the package of cigarettes for the change. It added up after a few trips. I was about seven or eight years old. Her friend was small like me. She gave me some of her unwanted clothes, which was always like Christmas for me.

Momma found a new reason to whip me. She wanted me to clean the bathtub ring after I bathed. I would wipe the tub with my face towel, but it wouldn't remove the ring around the tub, so I used Comet cleanser. This got the job done, but I didn't realize it would leave abrasive stuff on the bottom. She asked what I used, and I said nothing because I knew that however I answered, it would be the wrong answer. I would have another reason to visit the confessional booth on Sunday. Forty-years later I would discover using the bath bar of soap to clean the tub would leave no tell-tale signs. Why didn't Momma tell me that?

I never thought much about the red-and-white plastic telephone booth with it's two clear folding doors allowing entrance that stood like a soldier outside of our only neighborhood restaurant or the nickel it took to make a call. I also never thought anything about the blacks having to go to the little window in the back of the restaurant to pick up any food or drinks they might order. Momma had a black lady that would come over occasionally to help her clean the house for a special occasion, such as a visit from Daddy's relatives. I didn't have a clue what segregation meant.

My parents got away with not having a birth certificate for me to enter first grade. They got the news that I had to have one to continue on with second grade. I suppose they got in touch with my real grandmother. Perhaps Toby was able to get his hands on the required birth certificate. I also had to be baptized again. Lucy's mother and father were my new godparents. Camille, my new godmother, gave me beautiful sterling silver and crystal prayer beads.

Second grade dictated a new lifestyle at school. We were allowed to wear pants to school. It was especially good because the winters could be miserable with exposed legs. My priority was to master the art of getting out of the house before school without waking

Momma. She was not a heavy sleeper, so it was not easy and hardly ever happened. It was just wishful thinking on my part.

The only way I ever woke up was by one of my parents. I didn't have a clue that she probably set the alarm. I didn't know what an alarm clock was. I tried so hard to be quiet, but the wooden floor would creak and make noises. I knew that when she woke up, I would end up crying. My thoughts, as I stepped up on my bus to get to school, did not include my red eyes being a tell-tale sign that I had been crying. When I was crying, I was brokenhearted and didn't wonder if everyone on the bus could tell I had been crying.

My third grade teacher was a mean, arrogant witch and definitely did not help my despair. I was always being put in the hallway as a punishment. Before I knew it, I would have a partner in crime. Mrs. Stevens used to pull a girl named Royal Blue by her bangs, which were pulled back into a ponytail at the crown of her head, and she would land right next to me on the floor in the hallway. I guess she was as bad as I was, or she thought it was more fun than the classroom and wanted to join me. We had a good time while being punished. No one realized I was more worried about the punishment I would get from Momma when I would get home, but even that didn't prevent my next episode of mischievousness.

By this time I had discovered all of Momma's personal items in her closet, at least the ones I could reach. Now, it was time to put a chair to that closet and explore the top shelf when she wasn't home. There was a pair of shoes that made my jaw drop. I had never seen anything so beautiful. These shoes were like Cinderella's slippers. They were a soft acrylic and had rhinestones on them. By the time I was able to get to them, my feet were bigger than Momma's feet, and I didn't have the honor to try to put them on.

I was almost seven years old and didn't know how to cope with my little life's problems. I knew Mrs. Stevens had a young son. I was compelled to wonder if he had a life similar to mine, or was she more tolerant to her own son.

The bathroom lavatory at home was attached to the wall with a few pipes exposed just below the bowl. There was a small space under this contraption where I could retreat and cover my head with my hands.

Sometimes, while Momma was whipping me and I was in a fetal position in this safe place, I could hear her mother in the background screaming, "You're going to kill her." I really did think she was going to kill me.

I had forgotten about the spitting incident, but in Momma's pharmaceutical mind it was fresh. Even though she never mentioned it again, her actions spoke volumes. She was determined to make me miserable.

Momma had pills for every occasion – headaches, nausea, diarrhea, pain, constipation, depression, migraines, lack of sleep, or whatever else you could come up with. I'm surprised she was able to take care of us as well as she did. Perhaps the cooking of meals and laundering our clothes was overwhelming for her. Her favorite saying was that she worked like a dog. I was so tired of hearing the same phrase.

When I left for school in the mornings, I always had a knotted white-cotton handkerchief with ten cents in it for lunch. There was never a penny more. For the most part there was nothing that required extra money until the 4-H club at school started selling popcorn for ten cents to raise money for a special occasion or event while we were waiting for the bus to go home. It was strange to see a table set up in the corridor between the gymnasium and the classrooms. I had never smelled anything so delicious, nor had I seen a popcorn machine. Lucy always had her popcorn funds and shared her popcorn with me. For that brief time before going home for the evening, I was in heaven. That was one thing I didn't have to share with Putsy. I was beginning to despise him more every day.

Funerals seemed to be prevalent in our family. Some of the older family members were dying frequently. We would go "Upfront" to different aunt and uncle's houses after the visits to the graveyard. Uncle Henry always got my little mind thinking. I would ask, "How are we related to Uncle Henry?" No one noticed my confusion and need to have an answer, but twenty years later I would understand. I enjoyed going to Fleming's Cemetery further down on the bayou. It was on a huge hill with a lot of mossy trees, and we would run up and down the hill. The hanging moss would touch our heads. I thought it was the spookiest place I'd ever seen.

If there was something to get involved in at

school, I definitely joined. Whether it was a play, a sports game, cheerleading, track, homecoming, field trips, or whatever else occurred, I signed up. It didn't matter that I couldn't carry a note. I joined the choir anyway. Momma always made my costumes, but most times we had disagreements, with crying and apologies, and I wondered if she would actually finish it. She would threaten me, and I would be concerned. She complained about her commitment the entire time. Sometimes she seemed so mad at me I feared she would say , "I'm done," and stop production. She never drove me anywhere to do anything. Daddy always delivered me to wherever I needed to go, except church. Daddy was not ever going to be found in church.

I was not a fan of violence or fighting of any kind. I cringed at the idea of such activity. However, Daddy and Paw started going to boxing matches, and Putsy and I would be invited. I believe my eyes were closed more than they were open.

Every Sunday was an escape for me, but for Momma it was another opportunity to torture me by pinching me instead of slapping me. For me it was a silent abuse. My feelings were always hurt and church was not a happy time. She wouldn't hit me, but she would give me eyes that could kill. I didn't have anything else to compare it to except for that wicked grandmother and her evil eyes. Of course, every Sunday I was in the confessional booth confessing I had lied to my momma. I stood in line waiting for my turn and was happy I got those moments away from Momma. The ride home from church was always dreadful, and I thanked God to get me home where Daddy was near. Momma was more agreeable and tolerant when Daddy was around. If it had been acceptable, that priest eventually should have come out of the confessional booth screaming, "Enough lying already," but thank God he never did.

It was becoming obvious that I was never going to have my real mother in my life again. I wouldn't say I hated my new momma, but I was always wishing that I could have a different momma. Was I beginning to think I could have the luxury of mommy number three?

At the end of November Daddy would buy a khaki-colored burlap sack of oysters. Paw and Daddy would put together a wooden table comprised of a door sitting on two barrels.

They would shuck and eat and then store and freeze whatever oysters were left over. There would be three holiday dinners within a month or so. Thanksgiving was the beginning. As sure as life itself, we would have a turkey with oyster dressing, a baked ham with cherries and pineapple slices on top, gumbo, potato salad, yams, black-eyed peas, cabbage, pecan pies, and pineapple upside down cake. I can't remember ever having anything different to eat for those holidays, and why would there be. My momma and her mom were great cooks.

One time, as Daddy and Paw began to shuck a sack of oysters, I peeked from behind a huge ivy-covered oak tree in our driveway. They probably knew I was there, but didn't lead on if they did. They were seriously concocting a sauce which consisted of ketchup, horseradish, hot sauce, lemon juice, and mayonnaise. Once again it was the cellophane wrappers of the crackers that got my attention. Also the way they would suck down those critters would make my mouth water, because it sounded so delicious. Before I knew it, my Daddy was trying to coax me from behind the tree. It didn't take long for me to be at the table and ready to be the judge. I waited eagerly to eat an oyster. I ran to the nearest tree to spit it out. Actually, it was more like flying out of my mouth. They thought it was really funny and had a huge laugh.

Whenever the pecan trees were blooming, Putsy and I gathered the pecans on the ground. We filled buckets at a time. Paw sat for hours taking the shells off, while Momma made pecan pralines and froze some pecans. Pralines were another one of my favorites. I would salivate as the sugar, water, vanilla extract, and pecans boiled and the aroma filled the air. I couldn't eat too many, but I never had enough. In addition, Momma brought half of them next door to Maw, Paw, and Putsy.

My momma's parents were born and raised around the basins. These were the little bodies of water deeper into the bayous. It was a place that had to be visited by boat, but definitely not a motor boat. The boats were "pirogues" which were hand carved from cypress trees. Maybe my momma's parents could have been considered swamp people.

Back in the day, they would barter food, so Maw learned to cook whatever was available in as many different ways as she could imagine. They were cooking whatever nature provided. Different relatives were always bringing over ducks, turtle, seafood, vegetables, desserts, etc. There was a season for all foods. Food was a big part of our lives.

I especially like the Mobilian Turtle Soup. Daddy would go into the bayous and set the turtle traps, and then he would have to go back for the kill. I waited in anticipation to see how many eggs were in each turtle. As Momma cooked the turtle, the scent lingered the entire day. By the time it was ready to eat, so was I. I liked to tear the shell of the little eggs open with my teeth, and then I would suck out the liquid part as well as the yolk, which was smaller and a little different than that of a chicken egg. It surprised me that I could do such a thing, because I was a bit of a picky-food child. Momma and Daddy called avocados an alligator pear. I suppose this was because of the lumpiness of the peeling. I was not about to eat anything that was green. I wouldn't even eat carrot cake. It didn't sound like anything I wanted going down my neck.

Daddy always had his own garden of vegetables, and we always looked forward to okra season, when Momma made chicken or seafood gumbo. He also grew parsley, green beans, squash, corn, and eggplant. Daddy raised chickens for the eggs, and many times Momma even cooked one of the hens. I wouldn't watch Daddy ring the chicken's neck, but I did watch the plucking of the feathers and sometimes pulled a few myself.

Once or twice I had the opportunity to see a snake swallow a chicken egg whole. This was very gross. Any time Daddy heard the chickens make a particular commotion, he would run to the chicken coop, knowing it probably was a snake. If it didn't have two legs and walked, Momma was afraid of it. If ever there was a mouse or a rat in the house, Momma would not rest until Daddy told her he killed it. She did not want to see it dead or alive.

I never noticed the lack of affection between Momma and Daddy. Neither of my parents was ever waiting with open arms and a hug at the front door. I did notice that every time we went to visit some relatives, they always fought on the trip home. It was always when Momma had a few drinks. I never knew why they were arguing, but it was consistent and it terrified me. I was always hoping things would be better in the morning.

If Momma had any type of complaint or issue, she would write a note or sometimes a letter to Daddy before she went to sleep. It seemed like every other day, if not every day. After a few days went by, things would get back to normal. However, the physical abuse to me never stopped. There was always consistent drama.

I'll never forget Lucy breaking the news to me that she was getting braces. I could not imagine what she was trying to explain to me. I would have to see it to believe it and did not look forward to that day. I was so disappointed and brokenhearted. It was at Lucy's house that I ate some candy occasionally. We would not be able to wrestle or eat taffy. Life would be very different for us. It was not because of this, but eventually we drifted apart. It was time for her to start having more friends her own age and in her class. She was a grade above me, and it was time for me to grow-up.

It was about this time that some new or long-lost relatives started coming over on the weekends. Uncle Ro and Aunt Val had two girls my age and two younger boys. They lived about thirty miles away. That was far to us. I enjoyed the company, and it was a diversion. Momma was in heaven because they would play cards all Friday night, all day and night on Saturdays, and most of Sunday. Sometimes there were as many as twelve or fifteen card players. Soon Daddy built a card shack, which consisted of a room with a card table and chairs, and it also had a very small room with a toilet and sink in the back corner.

It was the fourth Christmas with Momma and Daddy. I had heard of the Mattel Barbie doll. I really wanted one. Lucy got one. Instead, I got the Ideal Toy Corporation's Tammy doll, which made her debut in 1962. She came in a steamer trunk (which was like a suitcase) that kept her wardrobe organized. Momma made the entire beautiful wardrobe. She made the winter coat with a faux fur collar, an evening dress, some casual clothes, a bathing suit, as well as pajamas. They were beautiful clothes. How could I not like it? I never gave much thought as to why I got Tammy instead of Barbie. I was a little disappointed, but at least I had a doll. Maybe Tammy was a little bigger than Barbie and easier for her to make the clothing. Perhaps Momma had a more vindictive motive for not giving me what I wanted.

It was time for Homecoming for football,

and I was allowed to participate. It would be Momma's time to shine. I had to solicit for money to donate to the fund. The person with the most money would be awarded to the highest court. First there were the King and Queen, then Prince and Princess, and then the Dukes and maids. I ended up being the fourth maid. Putsy, on the other hand, escorted the Princess. Yes, he collected more money than I did. I was disappointed but not surprised, and I got over it.

Momma made a beautiful shrimp-colored evening gown for me. The dress had a single spaghetti strap of rhinestones, and the bodice was sequins made into flowers that were almost the size of a silver dollar. From the waist down it had layers and layers of shrimp-colored tulle with more sequined flowers. Momma even used a shrimp-colored fingernail polish so my patent leather shoes matched the color of the dress. It was beautiful, and I was used to being in the backseat to Putsy.

Uncle Ro and Aunt Val began to invite me to go to their house overnight on Fridays or Saturdays. Uncle Ro was a Wildlife and Fisheries Agent and had many connections. This meant he had a lot of invitations and opportunities to take his family places, and I was invited many times. Uncle Ro had jet-black hair, dark eyes, and a dark complexion. He almost looked Indian, but he was actually very Cajun. Uncle Ro was a lean, mean fighting machine. He was built like a brick house, as was Aunt Val. They were a perfect couple. It was a happy time for me. With four children, sure there was chaos at their house, but it was totally different than the chaos at my house. Aunt Val was blonde, fun, pretty, and wasn't sick all of the time, nor did she complain all the time. She was the kind of mother I wanted. Another great aspect of my visits was Putsy was not invited. As the saying goes, "Out of sight, out of mind." I was free to be me for a day or two. I really did feel special and normal when I was at their house. I would have preferred to not go home.

There was a park behind their backyard fence. We would go to the park, or we would go to the community swimming pool. We also went shopping and rode the bikes around the neighborhood. Going to the drugstore was even fun because at home we didn't have any of these places nearby. There was a rack of novelty toys for a couple of bucks. I liked the one that was a hard plastic straw with a thick gel that would be put on the end of the straw to blow up like a balloon.

My parents made plans to meet Uncle Ro, Aunt Val, and their four kids to watch fireworks at Pontchartrain Beach for the Fourth of July. I always had fun when they were around. Momma was on her best behavior and not fussing at me in public. Momma seemed like a different person. I became a huge fan of fireworks.

One weekend Uncle Ro had an invitation to go to the camp of a friend deep into the bayous, and we were invited. The only way in and out of the camp was by boat. At some point and time I remember Uncle Ro wrestling an alligator. He was sitting on top of it, and we were all jumping up and down and screaming with fear, fright, and fun. I never knew if he confiscated the gator, or if he actually caught it for himself. Perhaps it had to do with farming them, because they were on the endangered species list. The day was focused around a crab boil, which was almost a buffet because there were potatoes, sausage, onions, and also mushrooms.

I so loved the times that we spent away from home and with relatives, because Momma was preoccupied and happy. I cherished my tranquil moments, knowing

Momma was not going to be fussing much at me. She never drank a lot, but even when she had a few drinks, it always brought out the worst in her. When we got home, she was her usual self again. Momma would make up for lost time.

When we went "Upfront," we had to pass through this spooky place we called "Coquille." It was even spookier when there was a full moon. There was a huge turn in the road with trees and moss hanging overhead. It was in the middle of nowhere. I didn't know thirty years later it would be home to the Jean Lafitte National Historical Park, and it was on Bayou Coquille. I would never have stopped in that area, and I never saw any other cars stopping. The locals called it deadman's curve.

Momma and Daddy rarely visited Aunt Marney and Uncle Burke further down the bayou because he was a merchant marine working on an ocean-going ship and was only in town for a limited number of days. He spent more time offshore than onshore. I was fascinated with Uncle Burke. He was very proper and distinguished, not to mention tall and handsome.

Daddy started driving the school bus for a

different school. He started making breakfast for me in the morning. One time he put in front of me a plate with a fried egg, bacon, and a piece of toast, and I immediately started crying because the yolk was busted. He just shook his head and of course fried another egg for me. He proceeded to tell me I can't cry for every little thing. It went in one ear and out of the other.

At some point I believe the school counselor made a suggestion to Momma and Daddy that I start having a relationship with my real father, the father on my birth certificate. Evidently, they got in touch with him, because he started picking me up every two weeks or so. He had a younger girlfriend named Tina. Sometimes they both came to pick me up. She was blonde, petite, and pretty. I liked her a lot because she was fun to be with and probably not too much older than I. Before long she was pregnant. Sometimes I would spend the entire weekend with them. After she had the baby, I would help her take care of baby Toby. I didn't know he was the second Toby, Jr. One day I noticed blood seeping under the bathroom door, so I called for Tina only to discover she had cut her wrist in an attempt to kill herself. She was committed to a crazy house. Perhaps that's when Toby found out she was only fourteen. Tina was a lot closer to my age than anyone realized.

For Christmas Toby gave me a Jack Russell puppy. I called him Emmette. It was a Sunday afternoon, and all the grown-ups were at our house getting ready to play cards. Out of the blue my dog circled around Paw, sniffed at him, lifted his leg, and urinated on Paw's wooden leg. Paw didn't feel it, but someone noticed and pointed at the dog. We all died laughing. Paw just shook his leg and laughed too.

On Sundays five of us kids would walk down to the little restaurant for food-to-go. My favorite was hamburger steak with gravy and homemade french fries. It was the first time I'd ever seen little foil packages of ketchup. It even tasted different than the ketchup we used at home. The fried chicken and roast beef poboys with lettuce, tomato, mayonnaise, and gravy were so delicious. The french bread for the poboy sandwich was slightly crispy and exploded in your mouth, and the gravy dripped down your chin.

One of the best things about the restaurant was the lady's restroom, where a slot machine sat on a barrel in the corner of the tiny room. On our tip-toes, we could see a nickel inside the bottom of the barrel. We drove ourselves crazy trying to get it, but we never did, nor did we ever win any money. Gambling was illegal, so it was hush-hush.

There was about a quarter of a mile of wooded property behind Lucy's house and mine. Her daddy had an area cleared and put a huge picnic table there for special events. On the weekends, when several kids were with us, we would run through the woods. One time we were being chased by a blue runner snake. It felt great to run through the woods screaming like a maniac. At least it was good for my soul. I'm sure we screamed more than the snakes chased. Who needed toys. Had I known the trees above our heads had snakes in them, I would not have been there.

Occasionally, we would go to New Orleans and end up in a great place where we sat on stools at a counter facing a wall of mirrors. My parents had coffee, while Putsy and I had chocolate milk. We all had beignets. Beignets were delicious deep-fried puffy donuts with powdered sugar sprinkled on top. Cafe du Monde was on Decatur Street, which lined the river on one perimeter of the French Quarter.

I didn't realize I had lived less than a mile away from there five years prior. Cafe du Monde had only been closed approximately six times in sixty years, and that was due to a hurricane the day before. It was up and running within a day. I'm not sure if the sole purpose of the mirrors was to see the powdered sugar all over one's face, but they definitely served that purpose. I loved going there.

The only school award I seemed to be able to acquire was one for not missing one day of school in six years. The school would actually give you a certificate for such an achievement. I was working on perfect attendance for the seventh consecutive year. Daddy was furious when he realized Momma had let me miss a day of school, probably with the intention that Putsy could get ahead of me, as usual.

Before long I had a new best friend named Annette, who lived further down the Bayou. I was allowed to sleep at her house a couple of times. She was a lot of fun. I had never seen a spice jar. She used to put her pencil shavings in the two-ounce glass jar. I thought that was very cool. She also had perfect handwriting. I always enjoyed new friends, and as far as I was concerned, I couldn't have too many. When we were on the school bus going to her house after school, she said that her mother goes to the bathroom at 5 pm, and she would be in there for thirty minutes. That's when we would take her mom's car for a ride. She didn't have a license, but that didn't stop us. It was scary, exhilarating, and fun all at the same time. I couldn't believe what we were doing. Fortunately, no one ever knew. I certainly didn't tell anyone because I enjoyed living on the wild side.

Another one of my best friend's lived across the street from our school. I remember when their house was being built. I had never seen a house so big, and brick was also a new thing to me. She shared a room with her older sister. They had white French provincial furniture consisting of twin beds with the most beautiful and shocking hot-pink, tiered chiffon bedspreads. It seemed very "princess" to me and very elegant. Angie's grandmother was the other first grade teacher, and that's how and why they moved to the Bayou. Angie's mom was great, but her daddy was abusive. He hit and fussed at her a lot. She had a life a lot like mine in that she was punished all the time. At least he wasn't hitting me, most likely because he didn't know I was there.

Angie's mother and father bought an ice cream truck. She and her sister would work the window, selling ice cream, banana splits, and milk shakes, so she had a little money in her pocket. Her dad wouldn't let her wear makeup, but that didn't stop her from buying a Cover Girl Palate of eye shadow, blush, and lipstick.

On Friday nights we would go to the dance in the gymnasium at the school. Just about everyone around there was related to each other in some way. Before the dance we went into the bathroom of the Piggly Wiggly grocery store next to the house owned by her cousin. We were having such a good time putting our makeup on we didn't realize until we came out that the store had closed while we were getting dolled up. We had to bang on the store front window to get someone's attention in order to get the owner to open up and let us out. Nevertheless, we enjoyed the dance; however, the next day we both got into big trouble. We thought it was worth the grief we encountered. After our punishments were over, we thought it was funny.

In my life there always seemed to be great

adventure mixed with tragedy. Our school planned a thirty-mile trip from the bayou to the premier City Park in New Orleans. We were given strict orders not to leave the park area. Sarah, another friend, and I decided weeks before the event to disobey the rules and take the city bus to her aunt's house a couple of miles away.

While on the bus I turned around and noticed a black guy sitting in the seat behind us. He had his private parts exposed and was playing with himself. I had never seen anything like this and was very freaked out. I leaned over and elbowed Sarah to tell her. We immediately got up and pressed the buzzer to get off the bus. He proceeded to follow us off the bus. Not looking back, we ran as fast as possible, screaming like maniacs. We were terrified we would get caught by the school. We were worried that this incident might get on the news, but it probably never would have. Perhaps it even settled us down for a while, causing us to be on our best behavior.

Forty-something years later, I talked to Sarah about our escapade. She was able to fill in the rest of the story that I had forgotten after so many years. When we got to her Aunt and Uncle's house, we were out of breath, red in the face, and freaked out. She told them what had happened to us, and they called and told her parents. She got into trouble or at least got the sermon of her life. She didn't remember, but I suspect her family decided not to tell my momma because they knew she would probably kill me. Maybe that is the reason I forgot about the happy ending.

Sarah also shared other information with me that I had forgotten over the years. She says she spent a few nights at my house. This was unheard of because I don't remember sleep overs at my house. She said she could tell my momma was abusive, and noticed that she ignored us. Sarah could feel the tension as well.

Every Christmas Eve I had a birthday get-together, but never a party in which I could invite school friends over. There were always kids of relatives there to celebrate. I got used to Momma's craziness and learned to live with it. Momma didn't seem to like many people and certainly not my friends.

It wasn't often that new people moved into our neighborhood, because the properties were already occupied; however, to the rear of one of the few streets off the highway on which we lived and behind Lucy's house, there was a trailer that moved in. They had an older daughter, Dee, whom I became friends with. I was always interested in a new escape from my own home. Dee was fun, and we laughed a lot. I was visiting her one day while her mom was piercing her ears. I got the great idea that I wanted to pierce mine, too. Did I think Momma wouldn't see this string hanging from my ears? In my delusion, I honestly didn't. It was the first thing she noticed when I returned home. She had a fit and I had pierced ears.

In seventh grade I volunteered to help at the school crossing with the lady from Safety Patrol. There was no special uniform needed. I simply had an orange flag to hold out to oncoming traffic. Louisiana is still, until this day, under the Napoleonic Law, and we are the only state that has parishes instead of counties. Sheriff Al Cronovich of Jefferson Parish, where my school was located, sponsored a free vacation for all the school's safety patrol volunteers in the parish at the end of the school year. There were three hundred thirty-five boys and five girls. We had several cars on *The Southerner* train designated for our group, which departed from New Orleans on July 14, 1969, at 6:45

am and arrived at 8 am the next morning in New York City. We would be there five days. We stayed at the Hotel Edison at 46th & 47th Streets just west of Broadway, and in Washington D.C. we stayed at the Hotel Harrington.

Before we even got to New York, one boy was reclining in his seat asleep with his mouth open. Some other boys emptied a packet of sugar in his mouth. We thought he was going to choke to death, but he didn't and he recovered. It was outrageous and a bit hysterical once he caught his breath. We even had a huge pillow fight, and the train car was an explosion of feathers. I had never seen so many feathers in all of my life. We had so much fun. We couldn't believe how bad these boys were. The minute the boys got into their rooms on the twelfth floor, they dropped a water balloon out of the window. Immediately, security was knocking at their door. These boys from "Upfront" were out of control.

Our first tour was at the Lincoln Memorial. We then proceeded to the Jefferson Memorial, the Washington Monument, and the White House, including the Oval Office. We went on a tour of the F.B.I. Building, visited the

National Archives Building, and were there for the Changing of Guards at the Tomb of the Unknown Soldier and Kennedy's resting place. The Lincoln Ford Theater and the Smithsonian Institute were also included. It was exciting to go to the Bureau of Engraving and Printing, where they printed paper money. I thought maybe we would get samples. All I could see were dollar signs in my eyes, but that's as far as it went. I really liked the hustle and bustle of Chinatown. We also toured the National Historical Wax Museum, the Statue of Liberty, the Museum of Natural History, the Planetarium, the Empire State Building, Radio City Music Hall, The Rockettes, St. Patrick's Cathedral, and the United Nations Building. Forty-five years later and after reminiscing about this extravagant vacation, I couldn't help but wonder why Central Park was not on our list of touring, since perhaps it was the only iconic place we didn't visit. The most memorable part of the tour that didn't involve a boy was when we walked up the Statue of Liberty and stood in the head or visor area at the very top, where we looked out over the entire city.

On the second day of the trip, I had a boyfriend, which meant we would hang out together, hold hands, eat together, and enjoy each other's company, but we never kissed. He was so cute and different looking than the boys at my school. Russell had blonde hair, blue eyes, a light completion, and a silver tooth in the front caused by his sister hitting him in the mouth with her hairbrush, breaking his tooth. He was so nice. He bought me a cute stuffed animal, a dog that in some weird way looked like a deputy. It was about fifteen inches high, and it was grey and white and dressed in a suit. I called it "Deputy Dog." I kept the souvenir for a long time. I had never been given such a gift from a boy. We didn't last very long after the trip, but I became friends with his sister Carrie – a wild-child and a city girl.

Momma had gone to play bingo one night. I don't know what possessed me, but I asked Daddy if we could go get Carrie to sleep over. In a tacit way, perhaps, we thought Momma would just let her sleep over without any argument. However, when Momma got home, she pitched the biggest fit ever. She made us take my friend home at 10:30 pm. We were so embarrassed. Daddy was the maddest I'd ever seen him.

Chapter Three
The Fire Hall on the Bayou

Not long after that incident, Daddy decided to separate from Momma. He had an offer to take the position of Fire Chief further down the bayou, located very close to the school I attended. It would give Daddy an excuse to leave, and I would go live with him. There were living quarters in the back of the fire hall. We were both fed up with her complaining and chronic illnesses and welcomed the escape and relief. I would visit Momma often or whenever I wanted.

I continued to help the Safety Patrol lady the following year. Daddy's other bus driver friend who lived next door had a daughter a year older than I. Rosa joined in on the job of getting the school children across the street with me. It was her aunt that we assisted. She was a nice older lady. We were given another free trip. This time it was to Florida.

I had begun to visit a little with my biological mother again. I slept at her house the night before the trip. She was going to see me off on this trip. I began to pack my bag by simply throwing all my clothes in a pile into a suitcase. I was going nowhere fast and couldn't even close it properly, so my mother emptied everything in the middle of the bed and started rolling each and every article of clothing so it all fit perfectly and closed.

This time we were transported by five Greyhound buses. Our bus driver was so cool and a lot of fun. His name was George, and we called him George of the Jungle for fun. Of course, once again I had a boyfriend on the second day by the name of Pierre. I didn't get a souvenir from him, but I enjoyed his company. We went to Busch Gardens, Esther Williams Underwater Ballet, and The Fountain of Youth in St. Augustine, the place where Ponce de Leon supposedly discovered Florida.

I didn't have the itinerary for this trip and couldn't remember the other iconic places we toured, but forty-three years later Rosa told me we went to the Kennedy Space Center in Cape Canaveral, the Florida Caverns State Park near Marianna, and the Ringling Bros Museum in Sarasota. Once again we had our plates full.

We slept at motels along the route we traveled. There was motel after motel, and they seemed to be endless. I'll never forget some of the things that happened. Momma created a vacation wardrobe for me. She even made a two-piece, cotton-plaid bathing suit for me. At that time there wasn't swimsuit fabric. My swimsuit even had a zipper. The main colors were navy blue and white, blue being my favorite color. So, I was ready for an evening of swimming. There was an extra door in the room. I had never been in a motel room before and had no idea the door adjoined to the next room. I wanted to know what was behind the door. I was standing naked, banging and pulling on the door, when all of a sudden it opened and there were a bunch of boys staring at me. No one, much less boys, had ever seen my naked body. It was an embarrassing moment to say the least.

Before we knew it, everyone had their nice, white, fluffy towels not only at the pool, but in the pool. The boys wet the towels, making weapons out of them, which resulted in them stinging each other. We were screaming with laughter. I even got pounded by a couple of towels and ended up with several large bruises but loved every second of it. I was accustomed to bruises; they didn't bother me. We did get in trouble, but it was so worth it. I'm sure the management was happy to see us leave. Who knows, maybe they asked our group leader to remove us from the premises.

A guy was taken to the hospital a couple of days into the trip because he had been sniffing oven cleaner and ended up unconscious. We had no idea about such activity and found it very scary. The only real problem with this trip was it didn't last long enough.

Once a month Daddy let me have a party in the big fire hall. My favorite thing was playing spin the bottle. The person spinning the bottle would get to kiss the person the bottle pointed to. I was making up for lost time. All my friends from school were invited. Life was great. Momma was not happy when I told her one of my older friends taught me how to shave my legs. What was new? She was always angry or at least unhappy with anything I did.

Another perk I received was an allowance. Angie and I would go to the Piggly Wiggly grocery store across the street from school to buy a Nestle Crunch candy bar, a bag of BBQ Fritos, and a Pepsi for lunch once a week. Daddy hung out at his bus driver friend's pool hall next door to where we lived. I never thought about it or discussed it, but I'm sure Daddy was also reveling in his freedom from Momma's doom and gloom.

Twice a week twin girls named Cheryl and Beryl gave dance lessons in the fire hall. They were cute as buttons and wore a particular perfume that I could have eaten, it smelled so good. I never knew the name of the fragrance, but I'll never forget the scent. They would put their hands on the floor and throw their feet over the top of their bodies so their feet were dangling in the front of their faces, and then walk on their hands. They were very talented. Daddy let me start to take dance lessons. For the first time Momma didn't make my costumes. Paw's elderly sister lived across the street from the fire hall, and she also was a seamstress. Daddy paid her to make my costumes for the dance reviews.

The dance teachers used to leave their mattress pads for class in the fire hall. One day Rosa and I decided to play on them. Somehow or another I ended up knocking the breath out of myself and ended up unconscious. Knowing myself, I was probably trying to walk on my hands. Rosa ran screaming to my daddy, and he rushed over to me and performed CPR. He knew what to do because he was the Chief of the fire department, and his job involved rescuing people. After hurricanes and on many other occasions, daddy volunteered for his community. Also, Daddy was a sergeant in the Korean War.

Rosa and I were always busy at the fire hall. There was a 1920s, wooden, high-back wheelchair. We would spin on the chair for hours until we were dizzy. We didn't have any entertainment, so we were creative and stayed out of trouble most of the time.

The library was just a couple of rooms

located within the huge fire hall. Mrs. Owen was the librarian, and we became great friends. Sometimes it was boring because it was not very busy, so we had a lot of free time. I read a lot of books and we talked a lot. The dance teachers and Mrs. Owen filled the gap that was missing from not having my foster mother and foster grandmother around all the time. Mrs. Owen's daughter, Tracy, just had a baby boy, and sometimes I would sleep at her house when her husband went out fishing for a couple of weeks at a time. I helped her with her baby, the house work, and kept her company. I adored her baby. After all, I was thirteen years old and wanted a job.

It was so nice to be away from Momma's drama, but there was a part of me that missed her. Rosa's mother was very nice, and I enjoyed hanging out at their house. It also gave Daddy some free time to himself. Rosa's daddy gave her fifty dollars to go shopping for school dresses for the new school year. We weren't shopping for me, but it was fun regardless.

Maybe Daddy felt sorry for me, so once, when we went "Upfront," he bought me a pair of red stretch pants. I was thrilled. I couldn't wait to wear my new pants, so I asked Daddy if I could wear them to go skating. He said I'd probably ruin them, but I insisted and naturally got my way. I tried to be careful, but the first thing I did was fall and put a hole in the knee of my new pants.

We didn't have a telephone until we got to the fire hall. A girlfriend was visiting, and we decided to let our fingers do the walking through the phone book. We didn't care if we got a man or a woman. We would call and say, "This is the electric company, and we're calling to ask, is your ice box running?" They would say, "Yes," and we would say, "You better go catch it." We were on the floor, rolling and laughing our butts off. Within thirty minutes the telephone rang, and since I was not allowed to answer the phone, Daddy answered it. It was the operator, and she wanted to know who was making nuisance phone calls. All we could hear was "Yes," "Okay," "Yes," and Daddy hung up the phone and confronted us. He was not happy. I said I didn't know what a nuisance call meant, and he explained that there will be no more funny phone calls. Of course, had it happened with Momma around, things could have ended up differently. Daddy was letting me get away with murder. After a long lecture we realized we couldn't do that anymore. We learned our lesson.

Two doors down from the fire hall was my favorite type of business. Rosa's cousin Julie, who was a little older, had her own snoball stand. The big difference from Lucy's mom's snow cones was that the ice shaver had three blades which magically created ice with the texture of real snow from a block of ice. She had about fifteen or twenty flavors, and I got more snoballs than ever. I was in heaven. My favorite flavor then became ice cream, which also had evaporated cream on top and tasted just like vanilla ice cream. I could have eaten one every day.

Before we moved to the fire hall, we always had to share food with Maw, Paw, and Putsy. So the first chance I got to buy and eat an entire cantaloupe, I ended up getting a toothache. This perhaps was my punishment for being greedy. I enjoyed it in that moment anyway. Eating the whole thing by myself made me feel special and selfish, and I loved it. I also had to deal with the consequences.

We were planning our annual July vacation to west Texas as usual. Daddy, I think, intentionally misunderstood Momma and didn't stop to pick her up on our way out of town. This was another unforgivable move on our part. It would be heavenly not to listen to Momma complaining and ruining every perfectly good day. We loved her and would have wanted her to come had she not always been sick and complaining. She ruined all the fun, all the time.

It was the best vacation ever. Daddy bought a pair of designer red suede and leather Cherokee shoes for me. Blue was still my favorite color, but red was my second favorite. He also got me a miniature trunk purse because he had never been able to buy me anything with Momma. I got Daddy to take me everywhere. I wasn't thinking I'd better have fun while it lasts because when we got home, we were never to be forgiven.

Maybe that's when Momma started dating an older man. I'm sure she did it out of spite. She made sure Daddy knew her new boyfriend bought her a nice camera in a slick camel-colored leather case for Christmas. Momma showed up at the fire hall with an unbelievable Christmas present for me. It was the first dress she ever bought me. It was nautical and fabulous. It had a drop waist with a navy-blue pleated skirt on the bottom.

The bodice was red, and there was a white blouse to go under the dress. I had never had a wool dress before. It looked very expensive and beautiful and was purchased by her boyfriend. I didn't care who bought it. I loved it.

Uncle Ro sold Daddy an older blue and wood-grain Rambler station wagon, and it had some type of luggage area on the roof. Rosa and I begged him to teach us how to drive it, until he finally gave in. Neither daddy nor we knew the challenge we faced. I thought we would all break our necks from jolting. I gave up on that clutch idea as soon as it started.

Eventually, Daddy ended up making a convertible out of the Rambler. There was a small parade around the Mardi Gras season on the bayou, and Daddy said Rosa and I could decorate the car and enter it as a float. I just happened to have a forty-five record of "The Birds and the Bees" written by the son of Herb Newman and released around 1964 by Jewel Akens. I also had a bee costume from a previous school play. We decorated the car, or rather the float, with huge green palmetto leaves. We had music because I had a portable phonograph. Daddy ended up drinking a little too much as we proceeded with the parade. I thought he would collapse or fall out of the driver's seat. We had a lot of fun and Daddy remained upright.

I was determined to learn to drive one way or another. I had another friend named Pamela who lived across the street from the fire hall. She had a single older uncle who had an automatic clutch. His name was Chuck. He was a fun guy and obviously as bored as we were. We would go "Upfront" to get a chocolate shake and french fries from this new burger place called Burger King. We would aggravate him into letting us drive his car on the way home. We would take turns driving. I loved driving; it felt like we were gliding down the street. I certainly didn't have those feelings as a passenger in my Daddy's backseat.

My foster family always wondered how my real mother always knew what was going on in our family. Many years later my biological mother confessed to me that she had a snitch. The snitch was an aunt of Toby's who lived a couple of miles up the road from where we lived. She told Ellie everything about us.

My parents decided to reconcile.

Chapter Four
Sweet Jeanerette

My mother arranged for me to go on a trip with her to visit my real brother out of town where my biological maternal grandmother once took me when they arranged my kidnapping.

I fell in love with the country and everything else there. It was so glorious not to be in the negativity that constantly surrounded me. It took only a couple of days before I caught the attention of the boy down the road. His family owned the only restaurant around that area. He was the boy in charge of steaming the seafood. There was an outside, detached room with a huge seafood steaming vat. I would sit with him on the weekends at night until he finished. He wanted me to move to Jeanerette, and this got my little brain thinking.

To my surprise, my brother's parents asked me if I wanted to live there. Andrew's adopted parents were so nice. Everyone called them "Ma" and "Pa." When I returned to my foster parents, I asked them if I could move and they said okay. Establishing a relationship with my brother was a good-enough excuse for me; I was going to be free.

I kept in touch with my new long-distance boyfriend through letters for the next two months. He could hardly wait for me to arrive, and the feelings were mutual. He would say we would live a stone's throw away from each other. As soon as school was over I packed my stuff and my real mother brought me to my new home. It was a little sad, even though I desperately needed to get away.

I'll never forget my foster grandmother crying in our driveway as we backed away and headed up the road to my new life. I couldn't say it didn't sadden me, but nothing would change my mind. Besides, their precious Putsy would still be there. I was sure they wouldn't miss me. I would miss my parents and would keep in touch by snail mail.

Until this point I had only attended one school for eight years. I would now start high school in two months. The much anticipated relationship and boyfriend didn't last very long. I was free again and happy just the same. A few weeks before school started, the new ma and pa in my life called Wormser's, the exclusive clothier on Main Street in

Jeanerette, and had their representative bring twenty-five dresses to the house for me to pick out five that I liked. This place was the best. There was only one other place to buy clothes in town. I was in heaven and now a fashionista. Ma and Pa adopted my brother when he was one or two months old. Now, my brother was twelve and I was fourteen, almost fifteen. I soon learned that Ma and Pa really were the greatest people ever. Many different kids lived there at some time or other. I think Ma and Pa liked to have a full house of people, and embraced the idea of the more the merrier. Pa worked hard and played hard.

Obviously, happiness was in the air, and the best was yet to come. I didn't have to make a conscious effort never to mention my prior abuse. It was easy to forget certain things as a kid. I was already having a great time and moving on.

There was another girl three years older than I living there. We shared a very small room that was converted out of a screen porch to a bedroom. There was only room for a double bed, a small closet, and a small dresser. It felt like I had the sister I always wanted. Her name was Vee, which was short for Vera. She was a beautiful girl with dark skin, brown eyes, and very long, shiny, black, straight hair that framed her face with bangs like Cleopatra. I used to laugh at her because she would unconsciously in her sleep brush her hair with her fingertips. She dated and would tell me about her experiences. She had a new guy every weekend. I thought it was so exciting. I wanted to be just like Vee, except without the sex. Sex was the last thing on my mind. I just wanted to have a good time. I even heard her having sex once. It didn't sound like anything I would be interested in.

Vee was just as happy as I was to be there. She had about seven or eight brothers and sisters in her childhood and perhaps not a lot of individual parental attention. We visited her mother and father every month in Franklin, which was six miles away and the place where I attended school. Her father's keepsake was an old cigar box which was his bed at birth. Inside the box was his little birth shirt, which was no bigger than my hand. It was hard to believe he could have been so tiny. I was glad he shared that with me. Some of her brothers and their families lived there too, so it was a full house with a lot of chaos. After visiting them, I understood why Vee would like the relative tranquility of Ma and Pa's. A couple of Vee's brother's lived at Ma and Pa's after they were married and while they were looking for an apartment.

We lived outside the city limits, where a lot of the sugar cane farms were located. We would go into town to get groceries, go to the dentist or medical doctor, shop, or visit friends. It wasn't long before I went to the Recreation Center with a couple of girls who used to hang out at our house. This was the place where all the teenagers in town went on Saturday night. The band would jam for four hours. The boys were plentiful, and I was the new girl in town. Oh my God. I had never been the center of attention like this. The boys I didn't get to meet and dance with the first Saturday were waiting for their opportunity the next week.

With my previous trips to New York, Washington D.C., and Florida, and being from the big city of New Orleans, I had a lot to talk about. Had I said I was from Crown Point, no one would have known which direction I came from.

One guy caught my eye; I liked his look. I found his phone number and called him a few days later. It seemed perfectly fine for me to do this, but Ma was not happy about the idea of a girl calling a boy, nor did she think highly of this bad boy. He wasn't really all that interested in me, so I moved on. I danced with most if not all of the cute guys by the second Saturday.

Summer was almost over. Ma was going to start her weekly beauty parlor ritual to get her teased bouffant hair-do – a process that took hours. Her beautician had three daughters. One was my age, one a year younger, and there was a baby. Ma timed it perfectly so I could meet Jane, the girl my age, with hopes that she would show me around school and introduce me to some of the other girls. Once again it was my time to shine a little because I was the new girl at school. Although I thought Jeanerette, where we lived, was a tiny town, Jane's family lived near the levee, and it was ten times smaller. It was actually on the outer limits of a small Indian reservation.

It seemed as though my brother and I were getting along okay and getting to know each other. At that time I didn't really know what gay was, but I soon found out. He had known he was gay for years. He was very spoiled and got everything and anything he wanted.

Pa was always joking and always clowning with us about the boys. He was a tall, lanky, and wobbly man. Pa was a perfect gentleman. He didn't seem to mind the long hours of working, sweating, and occasional miserable weather conditions. They worked despite the weather.

Pa's parents' Acadian house was next door but was separated by a field. They were really from the old school. They were up early with the chickens, had supper early, and were in bed before the sun went down. It was obvious Pa was his father's son and that his mother ruled her roost. They were both really set in their ways. They were referred to as "Old Ma and Pa."

I visited Old Ma and Pa whenever I wanted. I think they liked me well enough, but I always got the feeling they wanted to keep me at a distance. I don't think they thought too much of my brother and his bratty ways. They did not appreciate or approve of Andrew being so spoiled.

I had a friend Christin who lived near us. She also had dated my first boyfriend, but they had already gone their separate ways by the time I arrived. Unfortunately, she was a year behind me in school, and we only spent weekends visiting and having fun. She started sleeping over at Ma and Pa's. One day we were all sitting at the oak dining room table. Suddenly, Christin passed some gas. When it hit that oak chair, it sounded like a bomb went off. Christin's face turned a few shades of red, and I thought we would die laughing with her.

Pa always made me laugh. He teased me relentlessly about kissing the boys. He would hold a match box up to his lips and say that's what my lips looked like. This made me blush. Hey, the truth didn't hurt, and it was fun regardless.

One Saturday night when I came home from the dance, I could hear Andrew playing Cher's album "Gypsies, Tramps and Thieves." Ma and Pa were snoring in the room over the furnace and across the hallway. I knocked on the door, but he didn't answer. I opened the door reluctantly and saw him dancing around the room. The real surprise was that he had gone into my closet and had my favorite clothes on. It never occurred to him that he was stretching my clothes. I was furious and made him take my skirt and peasant top off immediately. Not knowing exactly how to handle that situation, I put the clothes in a bathtub of water. After the shock dissipated, I forgave him. He had a way of making up with me. Besides, he was my "little" brother who weighed two times what I weighed.

Once again, it was another memorable Easter. Pa went to Lafayette, a little college town forty miles west of Jeanerette. At some point it had the most millionaires per capita in the United States. It was home to Pupard's Bakery. Pa bought mini Easter egg cakes for each of us in the house. It's not like I wasn't feeling special already. They looked too pretty to eat but we did anyway. I had never eaten a cake that tasted like a wedding cake, but wasn't.

So, now I had friends in town and a personal group of girlfriends from the school in Franklin, two towns away. We all hung out in Jeanerette and loved the Jeanerette High School boys. A girlfriend who lived on the opposite side of the outer limits of Jeanerette had a 1965 gold mustang with a stick shift. When she got to school, one of her teacher's had yard duty. The teacher didn't know what kind of car she drove, so we had to get it out of the parking lot and pick her up around the corner. The only problem was no one knew how to drive a stick shift. We got the car in reverse but could not smoothly apply the clutch to go forward around the corner. I already knew I couldn't drive a stick shift. We asked this boy we'd never seen before to drive it for us. We were laughing so hard we were all huddled and crying on the back seat. I enjoyed living on the edge and being naughty.

There were three girls who rode the same bus as I did, but they were dropped off at a private school. One of them was dropped off at the Catholic School where my privileged brother went to school. They wore plain, white-buttoned-down shirts, pleated plaid skirts, and bobby socks and loafers to school. I remember one of the girls sat a few seats in the front of me. When the sun shined on her face, I could see the peach fuzz on her cheeks. I thought that one day I would like to have the same kind of peach fuzz on my face. Her name was Jolee. At that moment I decided when I had a daughter, that was the name I'd choose.

Just because I had a new life, it didn't mean my way of thinking had changed. I never felt beautiful, nor was I ever told anything remotely similar. I seemed to be above finding the beauty in girls who crossed my path. I was so busy dating I didn't give it a lot of thought. Besides, the boys loved me.

I had several friends at school but none on the bus I rode to school. Soon, a new girl moved in twenty miles down the road. She rode my bus. Rae was very pretty, with long, sandy blonde hair and a tan complexion. All the guys loved her, probably for her huge butt. I used to laugh with her about her butt for days. We became good friends.

Sunday was Ma's day off from cooking. We would order take-out food from the Yellow Bowl Restaurant two miles away on the main highway. Vee, my brother, and I would go pick up the food. Of course Vee was driving. We could hardly contain ourselves on the ride home. We would smell the aroma of fried shrimp, catfish platters, or fried chicken seeping through the bags. We couldn't wait to get home and chow down. It was delicious, and we didn't have dishes to wash, which made it even better. Paper plates on Sundays were acceptable.

Ma was a good cook, but her style of cooking was different than Momma's and Maw's. Ma would always pressure cook steak with onions, and I would pick out the onions. I really liked her meatloaf with boiled eggs in the center. She would also pressure cook different types of beans. And she always had a chocolate cake on the weekends. I learned to like most of her dishes.

It was my first Mardi Gras away from home. Rae was going to ride her horse in a small parade in Franklin, where we attended school. She offered me the opportunity to ride her second horse. I got in touch with Daddy through a letter and had him mail my Mardi Gras beads that I had stored for years but hadn't brought with me. I had never ridden a horse, much less bareback. Things seemed to be going okay until the end of the parade. Something spooked the horse, and it took off running out of control down the street. I was holding onto that horse's neck so tightly I'm surprised I didn't choke the horse to death. Honestly, I couldn't remember how fun the beginning was because I was so terrorized at the end. I was only familiar with running relay races and running from snakes.

Thirty years later I had a reunion with Rae, and she confessed to me that she had been upset with me because I hadn't help her put the horses back in the trailers. All I could remember was fear, so I just asked for her forgiveness.

Rae had a steady boyfriend in Jeanerette and fixed me up with James Rooney, my very first blind date. My date was fun and funny. He went to school in Jeanerette, was a member of the school band, and made me laugh constantly. Then he went off to college in Baton Rouge. We would later become better friends because Pa's niece Emily (now one of my best friends) and I started seeing him when we drove through the park to turn around, or look for guys, or just to watch the boats in Bayou Teche go by while we were waiting for some guys to show up. He lived on the street that circled the park. One time we convinced him to come with us to a fortune teller. Actually, we probably dragged him with us. My good friend Rooney enjoyed it, even though he was reluctant and only came along for the ride.

There was a little white church and a little black church in our neighborhood. Every Sunday my brother and I went to the little white Catholic church which was only about a mile away. Eventually, we would have the option of going on Saturday evening, too. I always sat in the last pew so I could check out the new guys who would come through the door. The confessional booth was a thing of the past.

It wasn't long before one Saturday at church I spotted a tall, slightly curly blonde-haired, blue-eyed guy, and I liked his stride. Before I knew it, we were dating. During the couple of months of serious dating, his brother was killed in an automobile accident late one night. Their mother was devastated, and it pretty much destroyed their family. His mother didn't really care for me. She didn't really know me, but maybe she was prejudiced because I lived on the wrong side of the tracks. You could not have convinced me of that. I thought my new family was fine. Our relationship was over almost before it started.

I had been in my new life a little over two years, and life was great. It was time for proms, and I almost always had a date. It was such fun picking out prom dresses. Ma always allowed me to buy a new dress. Every dance was better than the one before.

I always had allergies and was sneezing constantly. Lucky for me, there was a new pill that would absolutely knock me off my feet. I was sleeping before I knew it, but I wasn't sneezing. I'm certain my teacher was aware of my difficulty. My first class in the morning was history. My first priority was sleeping. I would doze off, wake up, and doze off again. One day the bell rang for the next class, and I didn't hear it. My teacher, who was also the football coach, woke me up after all the other students left and told me it was okay to sleep during class, but I couldn't snore. It was an embarrassing moment, but life went on. I learned to rest my head on my desktop instead of trying to sleep sitting in an upright position leaning on my wrist and hand.

Vera needed some extra money for more outfits, so she started working for Pa in the sugar cane fields driving a tractor. No one had ever seen a girl working in the fields. Her boyfriends, separately, would come by to see the attraction. When she got paid on Friday, we would always go to Mangel's in New Iberia for her to get an outfit or two. Sometimes I got to buy something, not that I really needed anything new.

Pa started harvesting field peas and did well with selling them by the bushel. He sold them shelled or unshelled. I got to do the shelling job. I would shell them by hand, and it took forever. Business was booming, so Pa decided to invest in an aluminum sheller machine. It was a simple contraption which had two roller blades on the end of a tray where the peas laid. I would push the peas straight into the rollers which squeezed the peas out of the shell and separated the peas from the shells. It reminded me of the old ringer washing machines. I got four dollars a bushel. So I started having my own money. It kept getting better. Ladies would buy two and three bushels at a time and freeze them for the time they were not in season.

It was my third year in high school. I guess you could say the time came to start skipping out of school. At the very end of the highway going out of town was a body of water called Burns Point. About fifteen friends, boys and girls, got some beer. We didn't care that it was hot because we didn't know about cold beer. We drank the beer through straws. Kevin was my best guy friend. Our relationship was strictly platonic. The party was in full swing by 11 am. Someone screamed "truant officer!" Everyone jumped in their cars and took off. There was a wharf on the edge of the water, and I had gone swimming with a few others. Kevin screamed to me to get out of the water, but I couldn't lift myself up. He told me to grab his hand and put my foot up on the wharf so that he could pull me up. At just about that time my shorts split up the crotch. I was so embarrassed I threw myself back into the water. Some way or another we all managed to get away. We went to Bayou Sale (pronounced "Sally") and continued partying. It was one of the most fun times I'd ever had. We were running after each other drunk as skunks and screaming like maniacs.

I wanted another beer, but no one would give me one, so I asked Kevin for a sip. I intentionally spit my potato chips on the top of the can. Of course he didn't want it back, and I got another beer. We were all acting like fools. My stomach was sore from laughing so much. It was so much fun. Kevin's dad's name was Houston and my ma's name was Thelma. We were yelling "sloppy Houston" and "sloppy Thelma." I fell asleep in the sun and got a bad sunburn. We had to be back to catch the bus home. It was very difficult explaining to Ma how I got a sunburn in Physical Education class when it had never happened before. She could not have dreamed that I skipped out of school. It was outrageous and so fun. We were so bad, but it felt so good.

Months later I had another boyfriend that

had just gotten his high school ring. He let me wear it. The first day I lost it at Cypremont Point, another water-park area. I felt terrible, but what could I do. He had a 1960 green Pontiac Bonneville. We stopped at the pool hall in town before he took me home. I went across the street to use the gas station's bathroom. It was a tiny room with an unpainted cement floor, but it had a toilet and sink. When I turned on the light, entered, and closed the door, I realized there was a critter staring at me. I flew out of there screaming so loud everyone in the pool hall came running to see what was wrong. My boyfriend went in the bathroom and came out with a possum by the tail. For some reason, he put it in his trunk. A week later he came to pick me up for a date and there was a terrible smell. I asked him what he did with the critter. He said he couldn't find it. It died in the firewall, and I was not about to subject myself to that stink. I broke up with him immediately. I thought, how could someone be so stupid. Anyway, I actually started dating him because he was a friend of a group of boys, one of which I had an awful crush on. I learned that was one way to get your foot in the door.

By this time I knew everyone I needed to

know. One weekend we had a large group together on the levee. A couple of guys had their boats, a couple had motorcycles, and several people had cars.

Everyone was skiing, so I decided to give it a try, even though I was not dressed appropriately. I had shorts and a tank top but that was not going to stop me. When it was my turn, and I came up out of the water on skis, my tank top was over my face, and my bra was exposed. I was so embarrassed but couldn't figure out how to pull it down, so I dropped back into the water.

It was my first time on a motorcycle. I didn't even think I had to ask Ma if it was okay. I was living in the moment. What she didn't know wouldn't hurt her, and she definitely would not have allowed it. She never would had known had it not been for the silver-dollar-size muffler burn on my left calf.

If all of that wasn't enough, a guy friend was handing me his huge set of keys which operated everything he owned. As I went to receive them, the key ring slipped through my fingers, and we watched the entire set of keys fall through the boards which made up the wharf. He dove into the water but never found the keys. I felt bad. With all of my friends and with all of the fun and all of the drama, it was one of the rare occasions to be punished which made me sad, but it was so worth the cause.

Pa decided to get a pool table. It didn't matter that nothing else fit in the living room. A pool table was going to change my life completely. I now had a reason to invite any guy over, and he would not be able to resist. Vee and I had guys coming and going. We both agreed there couldn't be too many guys for us.

Soon I found out that the guy I had the new crush on was Christin's cousin. I couldn't believe it. We would go visit her aunt, and I would sometimes get to spy on Clint while he was sleeping. I don't think he had a job, so he and his guy friends stayed out late at night and slept late. I thought I was madly in love with Clint.

Everyone thought Clint was hot. He had his eyes on a girl whose dad owned a store which also sold jewelry. We used to hear about Stephanie giving him money, jewelry, and even a motorcycle. Seemed he had her wrapped around his finger. At sixteen I wasn't thinking about any of the dysfunction of Clint and Stephanie's relationship. I didn't care; I wanted to be his girlfriend.

The boys in his group would wear the bottom of their tight white or blue jeans inside their calf-high boots. Their hair would hang in their eyes. I loved that straggly look. One time I ended up with an opportunity to smooch in a barn on a pile of hay with Clint. It was the wintertime. As soon as I walked in the door when I got home, my brother informed me that there was hay all over the back of my coat. Thank God Ma didn't see those tell-tale signs. I would have had a lot of explaining to do and definitely would have gotten punished.

Clint's brother Robbie was dating another best friend of mine. For some reason Ladonna and Robbie broke up, and he didn't have a date for the prom, and neither did I. So, we decided to go together. I wasn't trying to figure out the future, but perhaps he wanted to upset Ladonna. Robbie knew I was crazy about Clint. I was not allowed to have a single date. It had to be a double date. We doubled with Clint, the one I really had a crush on. Clint being with Stephanie didn't really bother me. Spying was fun, and I had a plan in motion, which was to be there when they busted up.

Emily had a Camaro. My brother and I started hanging out with her more frequently. As an excuse to go to town more, we would go to the car wash and wash the Camaro to death. Maybe her mom told her the only way she could go to town was if she had us with her. There wasn't anyone else around to accompany her. We would cruise every chance we had. Emily even thought this group of boys and the two brothers that my friend and I were crazy about were hot. Emily didn't know anything about robbing the cradle.

We all ended up at Cypremont Point. a man-made beach off the Vermilion Bay near Franklin. Besides, it was free and free was good. Everyone else was swimming, so we decided to go swimming in our clothes. I guess we figured Ma and Pa would be asleep when we got home. I was wearing my new outfit, which was unique and racy for the time. It was an overall short jumpsuit and there was a huge red satin heart on the bib area. The kicker was that it was faux patent leather. Shiny is putting it mildly. The water was gliding off this fabric like water on a duck's back.

When we got home, the lights were out, and that was a good thing. When we entered the door and flipped the lights on, Ma popped up out of the chair and said, "How was the water, girls?" We had lumps in our throats. Ladonna called Ma and told her we were skinny dipping. As we were soaking wet, we were obviously not skinny dipping, but that didn't matter. The element of surprise almost scared us to death and was not funny in that moment. Of course, later we laughed about the scenario. We would look at each other and say, "How was the water girls?" and die laughing.

I got punished again. I could tell a feud was brewing with that friend. Ladonna knew I was madly in love with Clint and not Robbie. I believe Ladonna may have already known that she was pregnant, and it was Robbie's baby. For whatever reason, they never married.

I had forgotten about my past life. Now my life was finally and absolutely so perfect except for my relationship with my brother. He was so weird. He was getting very jealous of me. In his eyes it probably looked like I was perfect and he was hopeless. I was beginning to love my brother and certainly loved being in Jeanerette more. However, he was a pain in the butt. Ma would have him watching over me like a hawk. And if I drove anywhere, he had to be with me. He wouldn't do any chores, slept late, had a problem getting up for school, and spent money like it was going out of style or as though it grew on trees. All he did was eat, sleep, and sing and dance around his room. He would run up a huge telephone bill every month calling movie stars. I believe his favorite celebrities were Bobby Sherman and Cher. He would always talk about how he was going to be a movie star and very famous one day and how rich he was going to be.

I went to many proms and high school dances. The prom that sticks out the most was the ultimate. Several of my really close girlfriends from school and a couple from another school attended. I was in the bathroom with Jane, who lived near the Indian reservation. I was looking at her orchid corsage attached to the shoulder of her dress because most of us had carnation corsages which we wore on our wrist. I realized there was only ribbon, so I pointed it out to her, and I thought she would cry a river. I'm almost positive she intended to press the corsage in wax paper to put in her scrapbook to have and to hold forever. Jane and her boyfriend already had plans to marry and live happily ever after.

Later that night after several cocktails, someone came to me and said my brother just hit two cars on Main Street and another car as he turned the corner. I laughed and said that's not possible because my brother neither has a license nor does he drive. Besides, he was at home asleep. Little did I know he did not need a license to drive, and he was on the run. I went home and Pa and I waited to hear from the police. We had to drive to Lake Charles, Louisiana, to get my brother out of jail and to retrieve the truck. I never did find out why he pulled that stunt. It was probably simply because he could and the fact he had never been punished and didn't know about consequences.

There was a lot going on within both Ma and Pa's families. Pa's daddy had recently died. Ma's mother had cancer and was dying. My brother was acting like a buffoon and was really out of control. And maybe I was a little more adventurous than they thought they could handle. It absolutely floored me when Ma and Pa told me I would have to return to my foster parents in New Orleans.

It could not have happened at a worse time. That one move I'm sure changed my life forever. I distinctly remember feeling like my life was over. I was devastated to such a degree that I wanted to quit school, even though I only had five months until I would graduate. Upon returning home to my foster parents south of New Orleans, they pleaded and begged me not to quit and offered me their 1961 Desoto 4-door hard top Fireflight. I don't think there ever was another car that had buttons on the dash to operate the car. It looked like a cat and was big as a whale. I wasn't crazy about the look of the car, but I was excited about having those tires. It didn't take long to get over the embarrassment.

Momma was still miserable, but at least she was not beating me. She was very demanding and hard to get along with. And now she was using me to ask Daddy to do certain things for her because she had a problem with asking him herself. I became more of the housekeeper and dishwasher (which was okay), but I was looking forward to moving out as soon as I graduated.

I had become best friends with a girl in my home-room class. The day after graduation I packed my belongings and started my own life and my independence. We decided to get an apartment together. I had a car and she didn't. We used to go out dancing on the weekends and sometimes once or twice during the week. We always ended up in the French Quarter at Deja Vu on Conti and Dauphine Street. We didn't leave until closing at 5 am. We always had a lot of fun flirting and dancing.

My first part-time job in the last few months before graduating from high school was at Burger King as a cashier. It wasn't long before I was promoted, which required me to take the meat patties off the grill as they came through the fire to be put on the buns. After a week my fingernails were ruined and I was looking for another job.

Soon, there was a new community called Fat City being developed in Metairie, which was approximately five miles from downtown New Orleans. The new area would cater to many night clubs, restaurants, and eventually apartment complexes. It was new and fun, and that was our first stop; however, it wasn't like the Vieux Carre which referred to the French Quarter.

Much later in life I would reflect on my school years and how I cheated my way through high school because I could not remember names, dates, or anything. I had blocked out a lot of my brain power in order to save my sanity. I think I did okay in Home Economics. We weren't learning to cook Quiche Lorraine. Anyone could learn how to boil an egg. Even I could fry brown-and-serve sausages. I think we also learned how to cook white gravy with sausages. That was the first and last time I made white gravy.

My next and first real job was working as a secretary for an attorney. Fortunately, I had taken typing and general business classes in high school and could type and follow instructions. I worked for the lawyer for three years. My family never talked about college. I was partying a lot and looking for the man of my dreams in the meantime.

Chapter Five
Here Comes the Bride

Within two years I was planning a wedding and looking through all the bridal magazines for the dress of my dreams. I don't remember the name of the designer, but the dress I chose was beautiful. Momma and I went to the most exclusive bridal shop in New Orleans on St. Charles Ave. We were in the fitting room with the dress that soon would adorn me as I walked down the aisle. Momma took notes, and we were off to the fabric store. The dress retailed for fifteen hundred dollars, and we purchased the fabric for two hundred fifty dollars. It had a high neck line and the sleeves were shear, pointed at the wrist and had ten tiny buttons. The dress was aline, and there were appliques throughout. In addition, there was a train to match as well as a long veil.

Momma and Daddy were good sports. They let me invite Toby and Ellie to my wedding. Surprisingly enough, Toby and Ellie didn't say a word to each other and behaved like perfect adults. A few months later my real mother told me at the wedding reception that Momma told her, "I guess we won't have anything to fight about anymore." Ellie had the nerve to say, "Yes, we will, there will be grandchildren." I was disturbed about Ellie's ungratefulness and her need to argue or have the last word.

My husband was in college to become a pharmacist like his father. Before long he dropped out of school and started working in the automotive industry. In the beginning marriage was a little fun, but as time went on, I became very disenchanted. Halfway into the marriage I'd asked my husband if I could go to Floral School. He didn't think it was a good idea. I wouldn't make enough money to supplement our income. I was very disappointed and didn't feel validated.

Just before we were separated, we had taken a vacation to Acapulco and Mexico City. We fought about everything. It was the second most miserable time of my life. He said it was black; I said it was white. He wanted to go here; I wanted to go there. We could not agree on anything. The only fun or rather funny part was when Montezuma's revenge visited him.

We were at breakfast and this look came over his face as he was exiting the restaurant.

He made a mad dash heading towards the men's room. When he returned fifteen minutes later looking like death, he said as he swung the door open in a rush to get to the toilet, the attendant's eyes were growing huge, as the look on his face was one of hysteria. The little Mexican attendant was saying "Ay Chihuahua." Maybe it was at this point that things were more tolerable for me because I finally got a chance to laugh. Acapulco was so beautiful, even though we weren't getting along. I was so happy to be back home. I could get away from my ball and chain.

Soon after our return my husband started talking about having a baby. I was looking for a way out. I obviously didn't think things were going as well as he did, so I moved out and he filed for a divorce. The marriage ended in 1978, painlessly and quickly. No harm done. Marriage was nothing like I thought it should be. He remarried before the year was over and had a baby soon after, and I was happy for him. It seemed as though he didn't care whom he was married to. He just wanted to have a baby.

My immediate problem was dealing with the fact that, because of a divorce, my religious status was now over. One of the main reasons I felt that my marriage was deteriorating was because of my husband's refusal to go to church with me on Sundays. It was a rude awakening. I struggled to find my own spirituality.

Pat O'Brien's was the most famous bar in the city. It had been in business since 1933. It was three bars within one establishment. There was a piano bar that was fun for tourist as well as locals. The audience could sing along with the pianist. There was a smaller bar across the hallway which had a long bar with stools and a jukebox. There was the entire patio area which had a huge fountain with a gas fire ring in the center where it was blazing and romantic and was graced with wrought-iron patio tables and chairs. The weekends were popular for the college kids and always guaranteed a packed house.

Once again I was free and it felt good. I could do whatever I wanted to do, whenever I wanted to do it. I suppose you could say, "I was my mother's daughter." I started working at Pat Obrien's two or three days a week as a camera girl taking pictures of the tourists and local patrons. I enjoyed making more money. I had the opportunity to take pictures of two celebrities, Chip Carter and another one of Miss Universe, 1981.

I wanted to live in the French Quarter, and so I did. I could walk to work. Sound familiar? Fact is, I moved into a slave-quarter apartment with a loft bedroom right behind my favorite club in high school, Deja Vu. It was now called Clyde's Comedy Corner. That is where I saw Ellen De Generes performing her comedy act about three weeks before she appeared with Johnny Carson, her great beginning. She was funny and a great comedian.

I was dating this very tall red-headed guy that I met at the pool hall I was working at a few nights a week. Red was wild and even wilder when he drank. The first night at my new apartment was spent sleeping outside the front French doors on the second floor balcony with Red. After having a few too many drinks, I was unable to get the door unlocked in the dark. The next morning this Spanish maid who came to clean the apartment next to mine was startled and concerned and woke us up. After she turned around and left, I realized my jeans were wet in the crotch area.

For an added decoration in my hallway, I

glued about twenty-four square mirrors on the wall. The second morning I was sleeping alone but woke up to glass breaking. I thought someone was trying to break in. I started screaming " Sam get up" when actually there was no Sam. I reluctantly went down the stairs and realized no one was trying to break into a window. Perhaps it was the vibrations from the garbage truck which made all the mirrors come crashing to the floor. I went back to sleep.

One night after leaving Pat O's after work, I was around the corner from my apartment and passing in the front of Broussard's Restaurant. There were several people gathered. It was obvious something big was happening. I was so outgoing and outspoken I boldly stopped and asked, "What's going on?" They said John Travolta was getting ready to exit the restaurant. He was the hottest thing at the time and "Grease" was the word. I couldn't decide if I should go around the corner to get my camera or not. I didn't want to miss him, so I stayed and waited a few minutes. When I laid my eyes on John, I melted and froze at the same time. I couldn't get the entire word out of my mouth. I was desperately trying to say "Hello," but the only thing coming out was "Hel" "Hel" Hel" without the "lo" as he was ushered into the stretch limo. He had a couple of beautiful blondes at his side, but that didn't bother me.

I also worked as a room steward, which meant I cleaned rooms on the *Mississippi Queen*, a cruise steamboat. It took several months of perseverance, but, with tenacity and patience, I finally was hired. I thought it would be like "The Love Boat." I soon learned otherwise. Each cruise lasted for six days as we cruised up and down the Mississippi River to St. Francisville and on to Natchez, Mississippi, and back to New Orleans. Every night we were docked in a little town and partied until the wee hours of the morning. It was a lot of fun but became old very quickly. I was supposed to be on the boat for a consecutive six weeks. Unfortunately, after three weeks I couldn't take anymore. The crew's quarters at the very bottom of the boat were always flooded with sewer water, and there was more drama than I needed. The *Mississippi Queen* was the sister steamboat to the *Delta Queen*. Once a year they would race each other up to St. Louis, Missouri, for the great *Steamboat Race*.

My next job was working at Fleur de Paris,

which was a French-influenced, exclusive dress shop at Royal Street and Pirate's Alley. It was also at the back corner from the St. Louis Cathedral. The clothes were exquisite. They also commissioned beautiful hats with flowers, plumes, lace, ribbons, beads, and other delicate trims imported from all over the world. They also had antique umbrellas, antique powder cases, vintage accessories, and jewelry, etc. On one of my days off Emilou Harris dropped by and bought a period top that cost fifteen hundred dollars. They also carried some new reproductions at more affordable prices. We also started a fad by wearing lingerie on Sundays. That was fun and definitely racy for that time period. I really loved being in that environment as much as I loved the flowers. The only problem with that job was that we were not allowed to sit for eight hours. Wearing high heels didn't help, either. I moved on to making more money and being more comfortable.

   At some point I went to work for an upscale wholesale diamond company owned by an elderly friend. I enjoyed working in the presence of beautiful jewelry as well. It was a family-owned and operated business on the seventh floor of a bank building. Rick was a counter salesman and was a lot of fun in the office. One day we were talking about New York. I told Rick about my trip when I was a teenager, and Safety Patrol Guards came up in our conversation. To my surprise this guy's mother, Mrs. Roberts, was one of the chaperones on my trips to New York and Florida. Rick mentioned that she had a photo of the group standing in front of the Capitol in Washington, D.C. Unfortunately, I didn't follow up on getting a copy of the picture, and I eventually left the diamond company and forgot about our conversation.

At the end of my twenties my mother decided to inform me that the man on my birth certificate was not my biological father. I couldn't believe what my ears were hearing. It didn't dawn on me that this very topic would consume my life. I was very calm about receiving the news, or perhaps it was more that I was in shock. The more I thought about it, the greater the desire became to find my father.

I had very little information about my father. I only knew the following: (1) he was a welder, (2) he also went to a union hall on Esplanade Ave. near the French Quarter, and

(3) he mentioned Colorado Springs. He said I looked just like Frances, his daughter, and perhaps she lived in New Jersey. My father's name was Henry Bojack, but that was not the correct spelling.

Now, it was becoming quite clear why I had the confusion concerning Uncle Henry in my life so many years before. I never forgot about the Henry in my life before four years old. Did my mother think just because she ripped me out of that life that I would forget the loving relationship with this man that she never told me was my father? How was I supposed to just forget everyone I knew in my life to this point?

Not long after my divorce, one of my first accomplishments, along with my freedom, was that I went to a floral design school. Since my first carnation corsage in high school, I was a huge fan of any kind of flowers. Who doesn't like flowers? It didn't take long to study and be prepared to go for the state exam, and I got licensed. My ex-husband was right. The pay was minimum, but I didn't care. To supplement my income, I got a part-time job at a bar and pool hall as a bartender. I worked the graveyard shift, and Shalen was the other bartender. We became friends and had so much fun. I started traveling out of the country, starting with Acapulco. I would sometimes go twice a year.

Since my favorite hobby was dancing and drinking for fun, I was on the prowl the moment I set foot on Acapulco soil. In my pursuit of fun I found the most interesting place to party. Baby O's was the hottest discotheque ever. I never had to wait in line outside and didn't notice that people were waiting to get called through the door. I would be there from 11 pm, when it opened, and stayed until it closed at 5 am.

I was mesmerized at Baby O's. I was in love with the idea of being in love and felt heavenly when I was there. I was a dancing fool and in my element. It had an arena-style interior, and the dance floor could be viewed by everyone. The aisles were positioned with little tables covered with linen tablecloths with a candle and a rose.

I would dance all night long and have so much fun. One night there was an Arabian Prince or a Sheik with his harem. That was the night I wore a light-green terrycloth spaghetti-strap full-length dress and high heel sandals. Perhaps between the jet-lag, the cocktails, and the total time spent on dancing,

I eventually stepped off the elevated dance floor and broke a heel. I threw the shoes in the trash, not thinking about walking barefoot into the El Presidente Hotel in the morning. I could have brought the shoes to be repaired. That was the good thing about being away from home – no one knew me. "Lebon Tempe Rouler." By the end of the night a bartender, manager, DJ, or a local had befriended me.

I was also invited to go into the DJ booth. This booth was suspended and hanging from the ceiling. This was something I'd never seen. The DJ could see everyone in the entire club. I was definitely impressed and privileged or at least felt that way. It was a great first night and a peek into an even better six days to come. I was really loving life and living on the edge a little. New Orleans had a couple of discos but not like this place.

A couple of days later I was walking down Av. Costera Miguel Aleman, which was the main street through Acapulco. From behind me I could hear some clicking noises. Suddenly, a huge stretched limo pulled up in the street on the side of me. I was taken back a little because all these people with cameras jumped out, and I realized it was the media. And then this special-looking vehicle stopped, and there was this lady with a blue suit and a blue hat walking off the steps of this vehicle that looked like the Pope Mobile. Lo and behold, it was the Queen of England. How was I supposed to know? In my panic, I did what any tourist would do: I snapped a couple of pictures. I was getting good with a camera.

Another time I got to drink tequila from a bottle that was handled by Engelbert Humperdinck. He was at an establishment that was managed by Javier, a guy I'd met and dated. I thought if it was good enough for Engelbert, it was good enough for me. There always seemed to be some excitement.

The next time I went to Acapulco, my friend Javier asked me if I wanted to go to my favorite spot at Pie de la Questa, and I couldn't wait. Pie de la Questa was like heaven on earth. The next day when we were ready to leave, one of Javier's friend's arrived in town to visit him and asked if he could come with us. Hey, the more the merrier. So, these two guys picked me up in a very ragged jeep, but we made it to where we wanted to be and the fun began.

Pie de la Cuesta was so fabulous. It was down a road between the beautiful lagoon of

Coyca and the Pie de la Cuesta beach by the Pacific Ocean. There were several places to enjoy the day on either side. In 1982 it was so not commercial. There was some type of military base at the end of the road. Parts of films such as *Top Gun*, *Rambo*, and old *Tarzan* movies were filmed there.

After being in Acapulco for several days and dancing the nights away for hours at a time, this place was perfect for some peace and quiet. They treated you like a queen. They would pull fresh fish out of the water and prepare it for you. We also went water skiing and swimming.

As we were getting to the end of the day, Javier said his friend wanted to know if we wanted to go have a fish dinner at his house. Of course, I said "Yes." But as we drove for an hour back to civilization, I couldn't help but wonder if I should offer to clean up after we ate.

By this time we were all worn out from the sun, boating, drinking, laughing, and the long trip back. I could hardly wait to eat and get back to my little thirteen-dollar-a-night hotel room to sleep. Little did I know I was about to get the biggest shock of my life. We headed up the hill towards the back of Las Brisas.

Yes, the place where everything is pink, including the jeeps, the swimming pool water, the toilet paper, the outside of the buildings, the plates, the flowers, and who knows what else. They advertised heavily for newlyweds. We went right through the security gate, drove around a couple of curves and into the driveway of this incredible mountain-top beach house. I think the word mansion would better describe this place.

We hadn't opened our doors yet, and the house staff was coming out of the house to unload the jeep. As we entered the front door, the aroma of garlic and fish drifted up my nostrils and dinner was served. The sun was setting, and things could not have been more beautiful. Acapulco Bay was unbelievably beautiful.

We got a tour of the fabulous house. My fondest and most impressive memory was one bedroom which was entirely accessorized with elephant parts. The bed had two gigantic tusks as the bedpost. There was an elephant-hair blanket and two elephants paws made into stools around a small glass table. Our host said his father was a safari elephant hunter.

The back yard was divine. There was a

swimming pool with a bar and stools within the pool with a huge waterfall cascading into it. The pool was surrounded by tropical plants and trees. I could have slept at the pool, but it was time to return to my reality -- my motel room.

The next time I was in Acapulco, I met a guy a couple of years older than I. Paco's parents were famous. His dad had been an extra in movies in Hollywood in the early 1940s with Bette Davis, Cary Grant, and Errol Flynn among others. He then went on to become a star in the world of movies in Mexico. His beautiful wife, even though she was older now, was a model in Mexico City years before. To this day I still have one of her elaborate off-white beaded dresses from her days in the spot light, given to me by her son.

My new friend Paco insisted that I move out of my cheeky hotel room and move into his house next door. I thought it was a bit forward and said we should talk to his parents first. The area was called Costa Azul, which meant "blue beach." They welcomed me to their home with open arms. The house was not fancy, but it was full of memorabilia. It was huge, with three floors of rooms. Some of the rooms were loaded with books. It was less than a half a block from the beach on Acapulco Bay, and it was within walking distance of all the popular night clubs. When it was time to sleep, I could count on hearing the waves of the bay. If it were up to me, I could have slept there my entire life.

It seemed like I couldn't stay long enough to fulfill my desires for the way I felt when I was there. The airplane ride home always felt like I was leaving a part of me behind. However, when I got back to New Orleans, I adjusted and was making plans for my next return trip.

About the third time I visited Paco in Acapulco, he had my arrival all planned. He even had a bottle of champagne for the event. We dropped off my bags at his house,where I was becoming a regular. We started restaurant hopping for the best margarita in town. By the time the disco's opened at 11 pm, we were completely wasted.

We were at the Magic Discotheque, which was basically around the corner from his house. We were sitting next to the dance floor and having a great time. The stools we were sitting on were short and had three legs. I reached over to give him a kiss, my stool collapsed, I fell on him, and his stool collapsed. Before we knew it, I was lying on top of him on the dance floor. No one was dancing, and we were the center of attention. We were dying laughing, and drunk. I'm not sure who started the humping motion, but the crowd joined in by counting down, "uno" "dos" "tres." The locals in the bar coined our escapade "a bear." I didn't have the nerve to go back to that club, for obvious embarrassing reasons, but I would see a couple of the waiters around town, and every time they would have a look of enjoyment on their faces. I would quickly retreat to somewhere else.

One trip home was especially memorable and funny. We had a stop-over in Dallas, as usual, after leaving Acapulco. I was melancholy in my seat on the plane, and there was someone in the seat behind me being fidgety and bumping my seat. I turned around to see if there was something I could do to stop the turbulence. There was a Mexican guy with a big grin on his face waiting and wanting to chat. He introduced himself as Jaime. He proceeded to tell me he was sitting at the bar in the airport minding his own business. When I walked passed him, he elbowed his elderly male assistant, Oscar, and said, look at the butt. I didn't mind traveling alone because I always made friends before I got off the plane. We started chatting and became friends. We were both feeling lucky to have met each other. He was en route to New Orleans for business for several days and wanted me to join him for dinner that night. However, I already had plans to be with my favorite New Orleans boyfriend upon returning.

The next day I called Shalen to let her know I had returned and to tell her about Jaime, the guy I had met on the plane. She knew his last name. How could that be? Katlin and two of her college guy friends were celebrating one of their birthdays at the restaurant to which Jaime had invited me to attend. I ended up having a group picture of my new friend, and my old friend, which was pretty ironic. Neither of them knew they had a mutual friend.

Jaime was involved in the oilfield business in Mexico and traveled to New Orleans frequently. I was always his chauffeur or available for whatever he needed. He was so much fun. I really liked him and always had a good time. The next time he was in town with one of his single employees, we invited Katlin to join us, thinking they might hit it off. They didn't, but we did have fun.

Jaime's parents were in town for a special event, and I was invited to meet them and several family members at Arnoud's, a popular historical restaurant in the French Quarter. I took a little nap and woke up too late. I didn't realize how it would upset him that I didn't show up. I wasn't thinking "Better late than never." That was the end of a very special relationship and friendship. He was married before the year was over.

The next Mardi Gras, Shalen and I were all decked out for Mardi Gras Day. I had a sexy outfit consisting of a black bathing suit bottom and a black faux leather jacket, black pantyhose, and of course high heels. She had a much more conservative pirate outfit. We were in the French Quarter, where traffic was horrendous. From the look of things, it didn't appear we would get to where we wanted to go, but we were going to try.

There we were with people on every side of my little mustard-colored two-door Toyota Corolla. We only wanted to go a half a block, and it had already taken forty-five minutes. At some point we thought this crowd was going to turn my car over. We were rocking from side to side and were very scared. I suggested to Shalen to get out the car and get the crowd off my car. I'll be damned if she didn't beat them off, throw them off, or scream at them to get off. Before I knew it, we were sailing into the basement parking lot of the hotel on Bourbon Street.

Our next plan of action was brilliant. We were going to crash a party in the hotel. We picked a floor and followed a couple of people. It seemed like the minute we walked through the door where the party was, there was a huge security man tapping us on the shoulders and telling us to leave. We left and proceeded to have a ball on Bourbon Street.

It's not that I was getting tired of Acapulco; I simply wanted to go to some new places. In 1983 I wandered off my usual vacation path to Isla Mujeres, which meant "Island of the Women," on the Yucatan. I had never heard of a youth hostel, but I liked the idea of two dollars and fifty cents for a hammock for the night, which included a small wooden locker. It didn't bother me that the mosquitoes nearly carried me away during the night, considering what was to come.

Hurricane Frederico was headed to the

Caribbean, and it was time to hunker down. No one was leaving the island. Fifty-to seventy-foot palm trees touching down on the beach was eye popping. Three days later I was very happy to be leaving for home. The ferry boat ride to Cancun was one of the most hairy situations in my life. My suitcase was standing up against the wall behind me. The boat was rocking from side to side, and the water was splashing over the sides of the ferry boat. I never prayed so hard in all of my life. I really didn't think the boat would make it across the water to the mainland, but it did. The stained waterline half way up my suitcase would be a reminder of my narrow escape from Frederico's fury.

I eventually started working at a flower shop in the Fairmont Hotel in downtown New Orleans, located across Canal Street from the French Quarter. The flower shop was located in the lobby, and I was in the middle of it all. I was the center of attention and would meet many new faces. Most of the time I was the only person behind the counter unless there was a special event or occasion. Our main flower shop would send inventory and fill in for me on my days off. We delivered flowers to celebrities who had engagements at the legendary Blue Room.

One day a young man my age approached the counter and wanted to order a bouquet of flowers for his wife. They had a room in the hotel and were visiting from Houston. He proceeded to give me his room number and his last name. When he said his last name was Pritchard, I said, "Pierre." He was definitely as surprised as I was. Yes, it was the very same guy I had fallen head over heels with on my safety patrol trip to Florida fourteen years prior.

A Sheraton Hotel was being built on Canal Street about four blocks from where I worked at the Fairmont Hotel. They were advertising for "Singers that Dance and Dancers that Sing." I had this great idea that I should try out. I knew the older girl on the second floor of the hotel in the salon who taught dance lessons in her own studio. I went to her with my brilliant idea. I talked her into trying out with me. The entire night before, I practiced by singing "Hello Dolly." I was feeling very confident. Maybe I thought I could fake it as I did in school, or perhaps I thought I could learn the routine.

When we arrived at the huge banquet room at the designated time, there were hundreds of applicants ready for their time to shine. They were instructing us to do pirouettes and double plies when I realized I was in way over my head. I guess you could say I did the back stroke right off the floor. With all of my childhood experiences, I think I bowed out gracefully and was laughing internally. It was a time before I knew about pride.

Chapter Six

The Hunt for My Real Father

I spent the next three years preoccupied with the search for my father. I quickly learned the meaning of finding a needle in a haystack – one that I would never be able to find. I hadn't seen the inside of a library since I'd graduated ten years before, but when a friend told me about the collection of telephone books of different states and cities at the New Orleans Library on Loyola Avenue, I made a mad dash to check it out. I didn't have a clue there could be so many telephone books. It took several visits, but I eventually went through every telephone book there was. I remember wondering how there could not be one other name with the spelling of my father's name. However it was spelled, I was looking for Boj-something. Was he in an old-folks home? Once again I had reached a dead end.

That led me to the old R. L. Polk City Directories. Bingo, it was my first lucky break. There was my father's name in the 1958 book. More importantly, I now finally knew how to spell my father's last name and my real last name. The spelling I imagined would have turned up anyway, so I didn't have to look again. It had the address where he lived at that time and the address that I would, for the last time, share with my mother. The house was separated from the river by the levee and was on one of the perimeters of the French Quarter.

We lived on the second floor of a neighborhood restaurant called Milly's Restaurant. It is currently a little neighborhood restaurant called Elizabeth's Restaurant. I, surprisingly enough, don't remember if I knew that my mother's gentleman friend lived in the garage apartment right behind the entrance to our back door. Fifty years later it gives me great comfort and a warm, fuzzy feeling to drive by that garage apartment.

Daydreaming about finding any relatives of my father was more like a nightmare. I began to watch Oprah. Every once in a while she would have a show about reuniting long-lost relatives. I could only wish and dream, which would automatically bring a storm of tears. I fantasized about finding his daughter Frances, and that was where the nightmare would gain momentum. I feared she would slap my face and proclaim she was his only daughter. Nothing was surfacing anyway. I didn't feel like my father's daughter and didn't realize how much time it would take for this revelation to permeate my body and soul.

In 1986 I started working as a mortgage researcher for a company at the courthouse in New Orleans. I was thrilled with the simple idea that I could check to see if my father ever owned any property in New Orleans. There wasn't anything. I also went to the only union hall I could find around the French Quarter, and there was yet another dead end.

A couple of years later the bottom was falling out of New Orleans. Businesses were closing all over the city. People were losing their homes and leaving rapidly. I was watching a news segment that talked about creating your own business. They suggested considering what you wanted to do when you were sixteen. I was having flashbacks of when I was about fourteen or fifteen. My foster dad pacified me with the idea of my own snoball stand. He even bought the snow machine for one hundred seventy-five dollars, but he didn't get the snow shack built quickly enough. I had decided that there would be very few hours to devote to a business after time spent on summer vacation, my friends, and other activities. We put an ad in the newspaper to sell the snoball machine, and that was the end of that venture.

Until this point I was only familiar with what the medical profession recommended a person must do to maintain one's health. Then I was introduced to natural healing. I was in need of some intervention and salvation. I was looking good, but I was not feeling that good. I was not about to kill myself, but I also didn't want to live, which was worse in my opinion. But things were about to swing in a different direction. I was about to pull myself up by my boot straps. My new life would cause a few friends to abandon me or minimize our friendship in the future. I never intended to offend anyone. By this time, it was all about me. All my negativity was transforming into positivity. I always said I didn't care if I was a dump truck driver as long as it was my own business.

Now twenty years later my teenage dream would become a reality. It felt more like a brainstorm. I was a connoisseur of snoballs. I remember living and breathing for the next opportunity to eat a snoball. So I decided I would move to Atlanta, Georgia, and open a snoball business. At the beginning of 1989, I loaded up my Honda Civic Hatchback and headed north.

My first thought was to set up shop in Atlanta but was quickly not feeling the love. I drifted northwest to the back roads of Marietta. Basically, I was lost, but it felt nice. Before long I drove by one particular intersection in Marietta and knew "this was it." There was a five-diamond baseball field screaming for snoballs.

There was a phone number listed for leasing information. I couldn't call fast enough. Because the strip shopping center was not completely rented, the management decided to let me have a six-month lease. It was the barest I'd ever seen any room, but that was not going to stop me. It had walls and a ceiling even though the floor was raw cement. It was two times too big, so I made a separation wall in one corner with several shelving units. I had a folding table for my customers to place their order and a workroom table which I had to assemble. It was raw boards and was heavy enough to support the ice shaver. For a little touch of color, I brought my huge Crown of Thorns plant, which was in bloom with little red flowers. I did worry a little about smaller children grabbing the thorns.

The entire fifty-foot glass window across the front of my store front needed something, anything that screamed attention. I didn't have any experience with paper-mache, but I decided to make a five-foot snowman. It took three huge balloons, a lot of glue and water, and about forty hours. I ended up with two huge balls and one smaller ball for the head and attached the three balls, creating the perfect snowman. I went to the craft store and got three black furry balls for buttons and a very lightweight plastic hat. I also got a nose, some red lips, two eyebrows, and two little eyes to make the face. He looked great, and I had him sitting on a milk crate which was wrapped in aluminum foil, making him six feet tall. It was the perfect advertisement in my huge storefront windows, and it was absolutely beautiful.

By this time snow cones became snoballs. The "ice shaver" evolved. This machine was like Julie's. It had three blades which magically created ice with the texture of real snow. I had become a customer of Bubby, the owner of Southern Snow Manufacturing in Belle Chasse, a company that sold everything required to operate my own business.

Within a few weeks the weather warmed up

and the baseball field was popping. There probably weren't many places that enjoyed having little boys walk in their front doors with their cleats, but I did. From the first moment I opened the front door for business and the first blue bubble gum flavor went out the front door, it was just a matter of time. The blue coloring would turn their lips blue, and that was cool. The kids were pouring in, and unless they were sleeping under a rock, they knew about the new snoball store. I was rocking. The entire neighborhood was excited. These people had never had such a wonderful treat. Most times I had a crowd four or five rows deep and even bigger smiles on these children's faces, especially after the games. They were as hooked as I was at five years old.

Ice was my major concern and dilemma. I needed a particular size to fit perfectly into my ice shaver. This was not New Orleans, and there were no ice suppliers, so I had to drive twenty-five miles one way to the ice house near the Atlanta airport to purchase five or six one-hundred-pound blocks of ice. I was able to fold the back seat forward and place a tarp to allow for a well to transport the ice. As I drove back, I could feel the ice shifting from side to side every time I even slightly turned the wheel in the curves. It was thrilling but not in a good way. I was on the interstate and cars were flying by me.

My first week of trying to get the ice blocks sized was crippling. Stabbing the ice blocks over and over with the ice pick was more than I could handle. It felt like my hands were getting arthritic, and I knew I had to find a better way. It was not my intention to attract a crowd with a chainsaw, but that's what got me through the chore. If that were not enough, I had to attack this hundred-pound block of ice in the back of my Honda. The blocks of ice had to be five and a half inches high by five and a half inches wide and by no more than fourteen inches long.

It made sense for me to come up with some other snoball varieties. I worked on a sno-shake, which was like a milkshake; a diet snoball made with artificial sweetener for customers that didn't want to consume sugar; and later a gourmet snoball made with ice cream, crushed pineapple, strawberries, chocolate syrup, coconut, cherries, nuts, and whipped cream.

About once a month I returned to New Orleans to get my supplies, so I was selling a product that was totally New Orleans. I was becoming very good friends with Bubby. It was a life saver to be able to reach him anytime I had a question or I hit a bump in the road, and there were a few.

By the end of my first year in business, I had a loss that would devastate me. Since a year before my marriage, I had a beautiful female German Schnauzer named Cher. She was my life, and I loved her more than life itself. She had been with me through thick and thin. She was with me through my divorce, which was not an easy part of my life either. The only bad thing she ever did in all her years with me was to raid the trash can over and over. One time I woke up to some noise. We had a large trash can in the kitchen. Cher was inside the garbage can, so I smacked the garbage can to upset her routine. It was only a temporary determent. She was back in the garbage can the next day.

I had her for sixteen years. Making the choice to put her down was devastating. The first morning I had to wake up without her was another one of the hardest things I ever had to do. I missed her so much. Then I adapted to the idea that I wasn't ever going to have another dog. I buried her at a place in

New Orleans where I could visit her grave any time.

I went back to New Orleans for the fall and winter and would return back to Georgia in April of the next year and the next season. The only problem with my business was the summers were short, and I could only operate five months.

I missed my Cher so much. I cried every day and visited her grave many times during the week. Finally, I accepted the fact that I needed a dog in my life again. I started searching for another pet. Instead of one dog I decided to get sisters, thinking they could keep each other company. I named them Ruby and Onyx; they were my little gemstones.

I had only had them for a week or two. One day I was trying to nap and had them on the bed with me. I had placed a vinyl tablecloth under the sheet in case they used the bathroom. I was sleeping and suddenly felt something warm on my back and could not imagine what it was. Ruby was standing on my back urinating. It definitely got my attention and got me up. Was this karma?

The sisterly love thing lasted about three months. Ruby was cream colored and Onyx was black. They definitely were opposites. Ruby was energetic and Onyx was laid back. Ruby was greedy, while Onyx was not. I would buy two of everything and Ruby would end up with both. When Onyx would see a bug of any type, she would rush to sniff it and would start gagging. This was funny. I finally stopped crying from my previous loss. These puppies kept me in stitches. When on their leashes, sometimes they would have me entangled and wrapped in the middle.

Even the toys that specifically were labeled on the package "durable" were no challenge for my pups. I started buying crew socks by the dozens. I would roll one and tuck it in and give one to Ruby and one to Onyx. They would take off running into the area of the house that I couldn't see, and within minutes Ruby would come back with both socks gripped in her little mouth. Onyx didn't care, but it did make me feel bad. Onyx was passive and Ruby was aggressive. The fact was, Ruby was selfish and self-centered. Onyx accepted Ruby for who she was.

One day when they were about three months old, they were running through the hallway in my apartment. I heard a thump and knew one of them had hit a door frame, but I couldn't figure out which one had the accident. About four or five hours later it was obvious. Onyx could hardly sit up straight and her head would bobble. I gave her some Bach Rescue Remedy, a very old homeopathic remedy which consist of four flower essences, and she was okay on the outside but would never be the same. She obviously had brain damage.

It was about 1992 or 1993 that the two loves of my life, snoballs and Mardi Gras, embraced. It was love at first bite. Bubby invited me to his "Magic Bus" for Mardi Gras day. It was a dream come true. He had toured a lot of the United States in his make-shift recreational vehicle and for several years had been parking it on Decatur Street just outside of Cafe du Monde or less than a block away on Fat Tuesday. Purchased and originating in 1972, the Magic Bus was a 1962 International step-up van previously used for the delivery of the then Ozone bottled water. Over the years the crowds continued to expand. There was a photo shoot at 3 pm, and everyone was encouraged to be there. The following year that photo was used in Bubby's annual newsletter, which was mailed to whomever was on the mailing list.

The night before Mardi Gras day, Bubby spent hours preparing for his mobile bar. He sliced lemons, limes, and oranges for the tropical drinks on the menu. The Bloody Marys were more like a buffet. They consisted of pickled okra, green beans, celery sticks, Tabasco, and spices. Bubby's infamous morning drink was called "Jet Fuel." It was coffee, coffee liquor, and cream; it was the perfect drink served over ice to get anyone up and ready for the hours to come. There was ice to pack, cups to load, napkins, straws, and everything it took to run a complete bar and to make everyone happy. Bubby was the host with the most. He put a new meaning to party animal.

There was every kind of liquor imaginable, and then some. It was a place to meet old friends and make new ones. It was also equipped with a toilet, which was very convenient and necessary. It was my home away from home for the day. I now enjoyed Mardi Gras day more than any birthday I had ever had. I can only smile when I think about Mardi Gras day.

The night before Fat Tuesday was my ritual of getting my costume together. Perhaps it began two days prior but never more than that. And for years I would roller skate. I never wanted to be the center of attention, but I was because no one else ever had skates on. I called them granny skates because they were plain white skates that laced up the front. They could be purchased for less than twenty dollars. I never used them for anything else.

My costumes were silly, the more outrageous the better. It could be a hand-me-down nurse's uniform consisting of a lab jacket and a nurse uniform dress that I cut and hemmed to the thigh area and attached a ruffle around the bottom. I would buy white stockings, a paper nurse's hat, and a stethoscope. I would have a sign on my back which read "If things get worse call you a nurse."

One year my outfit consisted of a burgundy-colored leotards and tights. I purchased a package of bobbing eyes and glued sets of eyes all over the entire suit. People were saying things like, "Hey, eyes on you" or "Eye got ya."

One year I didn't have enough time to get my costumes together, so I wore a beautiful pair of Guess jean overalls with a sweater and scarf. I also had a straw hat with pinwheels attached across the top. As I skated down Royal Street, the pinwheels made it look and sound like I was going to take off flying. The pinwheels were out of control and outrageous, not to mention hysterical.

In 1955 Mardi Gras was on February 22nd. I was conceived no more than a month after Mardi Gras. Mardi Gras was in my blood. When I was two years old, my mother had me sitting on her hip, screaming for beads and trinkets.

Prior to 9-11 the Magic Bus was even at "Jazz Festival." "Ed Bradley, the popular *60 Minutes* correspondent was a guest at the Magic Bus once." Bubby is the kind of guy who never met a stranger. Anyone and everyone was invited.

The next year I was determined to do snoballs again but had to find a new location. It wasn't as difficult as I thought it would be. Once again I snapped my fingers and voila: I had my next location. It was in a huge older mall that was more vacant than occupied and had many available store fronts. The leasing office was just as happy as I was to be their latest tenant. I rented a location which had previously been some type of ice cream business. There was a fancy upgraded counter across the entire front of my space. A lot of my previous customers found me and couldn't have been happier. I already knew the joy and happiness of eating snoballs.

I had saved enough money to purchase a huge freezer to make my own blocks of ice. At the end of my first year, I was unable to bend my back at all. There's no way I would have contended with the ice ordeal again. I was able to make all the ice I needed and some. This was a step above the first year, but I was in a dead mall and still had to pay the bills.

Several times over the years a couple of guys would come by for snoballs and inevitably ask, "Is this all you do?" I would say, " Yes," but I would think, You have no idea how busy this keeps me.

I hired a schoolgirl to cover for me so I could have a day off. I would always drop in to see if everything was going okay. One day there was a middle-aged man waiting to talk to me. He was a guy who opened four kiosks of a different snoball franchise in various parking lot locations. He also had sixteen kids working shifts. He said he had to come by to taste my Pina Colada flavor that he heard raves about. It was nice for him to admit it was a delicious flavor, but it didn't surprise me; I had the best. He was out of business faster than he was in business.

I had Ruby and Onyx in the backseat of my Honda. Onyx was trying to hang out the window behind me, and I was pushing her back into the seat. I distinctly remember thinking, you are going to fall out of the window. Before I knew it, she had fallen out of the window as I drove forty-five miles an hour. I couldn't believe what happened. Thank God there were no cars behind me. I slammed on the brakes and got out of the car and picked her up. Other than being a little stunned and having several scratches, she seemed to be okay. Once again I gave her Rescue Remedy, and she was as fine as she would ever be.

Bubby told me about a new "trolley car" designed to sell snoballs and got me in touch with the maker. I decided to go mobile. It was cute as a button, and I could see myself as a proud owner. At the back of the trolley was the counter top with a place for the snoball ice shaver. Below was a large storage area for cups, napkins, or whatever. In the front corner there was a fifteen-cubic-foot-deep freezer for the ice. There was also a small stainless steel sink for hand washing. Above it was the clean water supply. Below the sink there was a water heater. The trolley was made of wood. It was five feet wide, nine feet long, and eight feet high. It was precious and feminine enough for me with it's white-vinyl scroll lettering that read "New Orleans Style Sno Balls." There were shelves on the walls to store the bottles of flavors. No one was going to miss it because it was fire engine red with a white oval roof. Other than the creator of the trolley, I was the first trolley on the road. I doubt this guy ever dreamed that twenty-two years later he would have hundreds of trolleys all over the country.

I drove to north Alabama to pick up my new trolley car. It would be the first time I ever drove a trailer of any kind. I hitched it to my brand new red Toyota pick-up truck and away I went. I was not concerned, but I was going to make sure I didn't have to turn around. If I wasn't going forward, I wasn't going anywhere. I was trucking and couldn't wait to get it home.

As I got closer to home, I took the back roads. I was not thinking about the historical one-lane covered bridge I had to go through. As I approached the bridge, I was concerned about the height of the trolley car. I was so concerned that I stopped the truck to look at the clearance. I was entering with no problem, but when it was time to exit the bridge, that was another story. The trolley was not going to clear. The trolley was higher than the bridge, and I had to back up. I had to learn fast because I was also holding up traffic behind me. It took a while but I did it. As I finally turned around completely, I noticed all the people in the cars behind me were clapping. Later that night I was telling my friend what had happened. She informed me that on a radio station, they were talking about something being trapped in the covered bridge. I said, "Now you know what and who that was."

The first two years I rented apartments. The third year I found an affordable house to rent. It had a huge backyard and a huge garage. I could actually drive in the backyard and turn around as well. I could also park the huge trolley in the garage. This garage was not your typical residential garage; it was a commercial type with a loading dock.

I spent a lot of time alone after work. I would watch the "Oprah" show and sometimes she was reuniting long lost relatives. I couldn't help but cry knowing I was never going to find my father or that part of my missing family.

Being mobile was going to change my strategy. I started marketing to day care centers, school functions, church events, picnics, and company events. I also went to apartment complexes. I would also subcontract myself out to this guy who had his own entertainment company which offered magic shows, clowns, popcorn, casino nights, and other entertainment venues. He also did a lot of college events.

I had a huge following from my snoball business. When it was time to close for fall and winter, the kids would cry. My little customers never believed I was coming back, but I did. They didn't know how happy they made me. It was impossible for me to stay in business through the winter. They didn't know I enjoyed being there for them as much as they enjoyed having me there. I was only too familiar with the feelings of abandonment.

I had become a rockhound. I loved going into the mountains to dig for real gemstones, or as I describe them, "Gifts from God." Mt. Ida, Arkansas,was my favorite place to gather clear quartz crystals. I had purchased a rock hammer and was practicing with it. I would work my wrist, then with the elbow, and then from the shoulder. I was talking to a friend while swinging the hammer. Damn if Onyx didn't walk right under the hammer. I never wanted to ever hear that sound again. I felt terrible. It was her third serious accident. I gave her Rescue Remedy and she was fine.

It was the second or third week in April. I would return to Marietta from New Orleans every year in April. The first day upon returning to gear up for summer, I stopped at the grocery store to stock up. The next day it snowed. I had never seen snow for more than five minutes at one time. It snowed enough to last the entire week. I was looking out of the front window of the house when I saw my neighbors from across the street coming over. I opened the door and they asked if they could go in my backyard to see where the tree fell. Little did I know the tree had fallen through my garage roof. The garage was so high it didn't touch anything inside. That was a fine welcome home. I was thrilled to cook to my heart's content and embrace the snow. My puppies enjoyed the new experience of running through the snow.

Onyx couldn't wait to get from point A to point B to lie down. All she wanted to do was be in my lap. All Ruby wanted was for me to throw something for her to fetch. I remember specifically thinking that Onyx needed someone in her life to hold her twenty-four hours a day. She just wanted to be loved. You know those sayings, "Be careful what you wish for" and "Watch what you say." It wasn't long after that she died. I thought Ruby would be devastated; however, I believe she was happy to be the only dog now. It saddened me a bit, but we went on. Ruby now had my undivided attention, and she became a more loveable dog. She was a great Frisbee dog. She lived for fetching and catching. I enjoyed having a dog and never wanted to be without one.

It was now my fourth year, and it was about time for me to take a picture of my snoball trolley in order to have some post cards made for advertisement purposes. I got a couple of friends to stand in front of the trolley, which was decorated with a few balloons. They were eating snoballs. We took about ten pictures and only one was going to work. I didn't realize the little girl on the left was standing in front of the "S" on "Sno Balls" so it read, "no Balls" on nine of the pictures.

One of the funniest comments of the year

was from a little girl about five years old who distinctly remembered I didn't have blonde hair the year before. Her mother was standing beside her as she asked me, "Are you the same lady with the brown hair from last year?" Of course, I said, "Yes" as her mother's eyes got big from obvious embarrassment. The little girl wasn't finished. She wanted to know, "How did you do that?" I simply answered, "It wasn't easy." Both her mother and I laughed. Quickly her mother was leading her away before there was time for another question.

I landed a gig for a school near the baseball park and was hired to give away a zillion snoballs at this particular event. Evidently, a couple little boys had not experienced my snoballs. There were approximately seven or eight boys about ten years old huddled in a group. I could hear one boy saying, "snow what?" One boy in particular still didn't get it. Another kid said balls, balls, and he proceeds to cup his private parts for a hands-on demonstration. They all started laughing and then realized I witnessed the entire conversation. Embarrassed, they quickly scattered away.

My fifth year and my last event in Marietta,

Georgia, would be a picnic for a division of Lockheed Navy Air Base, which was held on a piece of property at Lake Lanier. I gave away four hundred six-ounce snoballs from noon until 5 pm. I charged them four hundred dollars and my expenses minus time were seventy-five dollars.

The first years kept me consumed and challenged. After five years had gone by, I felt the need to run away again. I was on a roll, so it was time to go. Perhaps it was that things were going too easily and everything was flowing – except anything having to do with the search for my biological father. I tried to pretend it didn't bother me, but it was an enormous burden as well as heartbreaking.

I heard about a company that reportedly found people for a fee. I paid the fee and thought I had a good hit. I called a man who shared the same last name as my father. He sounded older and in his old grumpy voice proclaimed, "I do not know any Henry," and abruptly hung up the phone. I was back at square one, or at least once again acknowledging I probably would never find my biological father.

It seemed as if I was fading away from the only parents I'd known. I visited my foster parents occasionally, but the phone calls became infrequent. I was having the time of my life. I remember thinking daddy's going to die, and I'm not going to know about it. Within a few months, that is exactly what happened. My foster daddy was dead for four months, and I didn't know. Was I manifesting these episodes in my very own life?

I decided I wanted to try to mend fences with Momma. I thought maybe with Daddy gone she would be more receptive, and we could pick up where we left off. I parked my little camper in Mama's driveway. Daddy had left behind a fairly big step-up van. She had been trying to sell it via Putsy. That project was going nowhere fast because he didn't even have it running. So, I had a mechanic friend come by and get it purring. I then put an ad in the newspaper. Within a day or two I had a buyer. We were on our way back from the title transferring process, and Momma wanted to give me a hundred dollars (which I didn't really want), but she insisted. She also gave Putsy a hundred dollars right in front of me. I didn't care if she gave him the entire thirty-three hundred dollars, but it would have been more considerate for her to privately give it to him. I think Momma really enjoyed hurting my feelings.

I had also witnessed the way she couldn't wait to put a plate of food in the front of Putsy when he visited. If he had a button missing on his shirt or if he had a rip, she couldn't get to the sewing machine fast enough. I didn't understand that type of treatment and it hurt. Putsy never technically did anything to me, but she made me hate him out of jealousy.

The last time I spoke to my momma she mentioned that she wanted me to send her a letter because she always wondered about something. All I could think of was her dreadful letters to Daddy in my younger years. I didn't feel the need to know what she wondered about. A few years later, she died. May she rest in peace. I honestly mean that. Now, both of my foster parents were gone. I had a great capacity to not forget the good as well as the bad. Perhaps they did the best they could. I did appreciate what they did for me.

By this time I was so angry with my biological mother for orchestrating this dark time in my life that I was determined to move as far away from her as possible. You could say I divorced her and never regretted my decision. I considered New York and also California. Realizing I would probably get chewed up and spit out in those places. I chose Phoenix, Arizona, which was close enough to California.

I didn't know how to get to Arizona, but that was not about to stop me. I planned this move over a six-month period. The East was about to visit the West. I loaded up my Honda Civic hatchback and headed west, 1700 miles one way. It didn't matter that I didn't know a soul. If nothing else, it was another mental distraction. New experiences, new faces, and Sedona looked like a great place to spend time. When I first arrived there, I was filled with my grand delusions, but I was quickly jolted into reality. That reality was I could afford to spend three days touring, and then I would make the journey to the Valley of the Sun, or was it the bottom of the barrel. Regardless how hot it was, it felt like Phoenix was awaiting my arrival. Several meant-to-be things were happening, and everything was flowing like a river. The move was anything but simple. I had to make many trips back and forth to get all of my stuff to my new residence.

On my first trip back I decided

spontaneously to stop by the motor vehicle division to have my license plate transferred to Arizona. By the time I was out the door with my new license plate, I realized it was personalized a bit more than expected. Ironically, my name was part of my plate number: LYN-056. I had not realized that the three numbers would, in the not so near future, have a more significant meaning.

When I'd finally finished all the relocating and was back in Phoenix, I started looking for a place to put all my stuff. Rents were definitely more expensive than in the east. Once again the river was flowing. There was a little house that I could afford to buy. It was like the house was waiting for me. I'll never know why I ever imagined this sad, poorly maintained house was perfect for me, but I bought it. It turned out that my initial intuition was correct. It just so happened to be about three miles from the premiere city park in Phoenix.

I inquired with the city about their licensing and discovered I needed to have a three-compartment sink and a hand-wash sink. I decided to purchase my second trolley, which would be in compliance. It was almost the same design but with less free space on the inside, and three additional stainless steel sinks.

I was starting to look for a location to set up my trolley to sell snoballs. I decided to go to the park to check out the possibility. After visiting the administrative office of the park where the "Kiddyland" operated, I was told no one had ever been granted permission to sell anything in the park. They agreed to bring up the suggestion at the next city council meeting. After a month of deliberation, it was decided I was to be the first and only snow princess ever. I had never been any kind of princess. I was thrilled and ready for business.

The little legal and/or illegal alien popsicle cart operators who circled the park were not impressed and didn't appreciate my position, nor did I theirs. After many failed attempts by the park rangers, the police, and the company I was subcontracted through to keep them away from my territory, I went on my own attack. I put my granny roller skates on and skated across the park to the place they were selling. I whipped out my disposable camera and started taking pictures of them, and of course they ran away only to return later. It was a hopeless cause. I had to pay for the rights to operate in the park, and I felt like they were stealing from me. And so they were. I prospered and lasted almost five years. Once again I made a lot of children very happy, and more importantly I was self-employed. I was living one of my dreams.

One of the funniest and most memorable incidents occurred when a little girl about four years old left with her dad and her snoball in hand and turned the corner of the trolley out of my sight. I could clearly hear her saying, "Daddy, she's a good cook." How could I not smile and laugh. I'm sure her daddy thought it was cute.

Other than at work, I didn't know many people, so I spent most of my free time alone. I was busy with home improvements most of the time anyway. I was constantly scraping old cement from the exterior brick walls, which had endured the southern sun and heat for fifty years. My poor little house was looking good after a fresh, new coat of paint. I'd been in Phoenix about one year or so.

I decided to join a metaphysical single's group. Every month there was a weekly calendar of events to attend. As the temperatures cooled down, they started doing "Sweat Lodges" in the mountains north of Phoenix in Cave Creek. I soon learned this was an old Indian ritual which was detoxifying and cleansing. I really enjoyed those Saturday nights under the stars. I had not been around mountains much but liked the feeling of being that high and disconnected from the world below.

I was already making plans to invite this lively group to my next birthday – my first party in twenty years. The main food attraction would be a fried turkey. It was the first time I'd done the ritual myself, but I'd heard of it forever. You can fry a turkey in about forty-five minutes by using peanut oil. I don't think any of my guests ever had fried turkey, but they probably never forgot. I even cooked a second one. This one was not cooked to perfection because a guy dropped my thermometer, breaking it into a million pieces. This changed everything.

One night while watching Oprah once again, there was another company advertising they would find people for a fee. I decided to give it another try. They called me the next day to let me know they'd found a relative of my father's. Oh my God, my father's nephew's wife Joan was anxious to talk to me. They had a daughter called T-Joan. What was really surprising was they lived in the town in which

I'd lived on several occasions near New Orleans. Of course, I called them immediately. I had just returned from New Orleans the week before and had just missed the opportunity to meet them in person.

Unfortunately, they didn't know much more about my father than I did, but something was better than nothing. It excited me to know there was someone else who shared my family bloodline. At first we wrote to each other about twice a week. It was nice to have the connection anyway. Joan was into genealogy for years and made suggestions for me to follow up. Since I was illegitimate, I didn't have rights to any of my father's documents.

Joan informed me there was also another nephew just north of Jupiter, Florida. I didn't hear any welcomes or acknowledgments from him or his family. I wasn't a pushy person and could not care less. Months later I heard his wife had a stroke and regressed back to a childlike mentality. It was his father who had been so rude to me on the phone years before.

Rumors from my father's supposed niece and nephew were that my grandparents immigrated to Pennsylvania in the early 1900s from Poland or Russia to work in the coal mines. They arrived with two children, a boy and a girl. They later had three boys. This is supposedly where my father comes into the picture. I have found supporting documentation from the 1920 United States Federal Census showing five children, including my father.

I can only imagine how tough life was in the early 1900s. It probably had to be worse for immigrants because I'm sure they only spoke their native language. They thought they were leaving their country for a better life, but this probably never came to fruition. There was also a tale that my grandmother tied the children to the kitchen table so they couldn't leave the house while their parents went to work.

Allegedly, my grandfather committed suicide by eating rat poison. Perhaps he had incurred some kind of lung disease, and that was his way out. Years later the mother and five children had family differences, and all the kids went in different directions and changed the spelling of their last names. The paper trails stopped, and there was no proof of births certificates, death certificates, or any other evidence.

It wasn't long after, I made a trip back to New Orleans and met my new-found relatives. I then returned to Phoenix. It was a Saturday morning a couple of months after we had our initial connection. I was on my way out of the door to go sell snoballs at the park when the telephone rang. I hurriedly answered the phone, and there was a female voice that sounded familiar, but it wasn't. I heard words I'll never forget. She said, "Hello, is this Lyn?" I said, "Yes," and she said, "Are you sitting down?" I said, "Yes" to humor her. She said, "This is Johnnie-Frances, I'm your half-sister." My knees were weakening, and I thought I'd better sit down before I collapsed. I could not believe what my ears were hearing, but I liked this surprise. At least there was a Frances as a part of her name, so I didn't have any doubts.

It was coincidental that we should meet, and it was because of her husband's efforts. She'd long since given up on finding our father. Her husband was on the Internet, searching for any relatives of her paternal family, when he found our father's nephew's wife in New Orleans, as did I. Johnnie-Frances immediately called her and was informed that she had a half-sister and was given my phone number.

There was an immediate connection. As different as our accents were, there was a similar tone to our voices. We shared a lot of background information. The parallels were incredible and endless. We both had pictures of ourselves in our dance costumes from when we were five years old. We were both married at twenty-one years old and divorced three years later. We both got custody of female dogs, our girls. My foster father and her adopted father both gave our husband's guns. After her divorce she began to travel to Europe, and after my divorce I began to travel to Mexico. She was actually a nurse for thirty years, and when I was sixteen I wanted to be a nurse. We were both born in places that began with New: New Orleans and New Jersey. And, we both had a couple of male gay friends.

Johnnie-Frances had recently left behind California and her husband in an attempt to live in another part of the country. He was not moving with the enthusiasm that she did. Eventually, he would join her in Kansas City, Missouri.

We were really making up for lost time. We wrote each other several times a week, and we spoke once or twice a week. We exchanged pictures, and I could see similarities to myself in her photos. I could tell right away that she didn't have the same feeling for our father as I did. As children we both had strong desires to have a sister. Now, we had Joan in the mix wanting to be the matriarch.

My newly found half-sister had a little more personal information about my father. It was obvious that her mother was more interested and inquisitive about the man in her life. I learned he played the guitar and was a rodeo cowboy in San Luis Obispo, a fact I was never able to validate. He was also in the 10th Mountain Division of the army in Italy in 1943, and while on the front lines, lived in a fox hole for days at a time. He supposedly wrote to her mother and was excited and expecting the new arrival. He even sent her two dozen roses before the birth, but he never returned to the marriage or his new baby girl. As minimal as the new information was about my father, I cherished it just the same.

Our father had deserted Johnnie-Frances and her mother when she was born. She did not have him in her life at all. Her mother remarried, and her new husband adopted

Johnnie-Frances. Johnnie-Frances was very happy that I confessed to her that my mother told me our father commented that I looked just like his daughter, Frances. Her mother always thought that perhaps he didn't believe she was his daughter. Maybe he wondered about the Johnnie in the front of her name. Who knows. Maybe our father didn't think she was his daughter until he saw me. Honestly, I don't know the answer. Even though we each thought we looked like our own mothers, we obviously had in each other equal amounts of our father's traits. I concluded that maybe we looked like our grandmother on our father's side of the family.

Within a month or so of our introduction, we both received the information that would be my worst nightmare and rock my world to pieces. Our father had been buried for ten years in Glendale, Arizona, a suburb of Phoenix. Not only was he dead and buried, but he had committed suicide with a gunshot to his mouth. This was the last thing I wanted or needed to hear. I immediately went to the cemetery to see for myself. More importantly than the heartbreak, there were some documents that the county had confiscated. They were the last of my dead father's personal belongings. I was the lucky recipient of these documents.

The most important document was an I.D. card with a photo of my father in his later years, his fingerprint, and my father's signature. There was his Social Security card, which for some reason was blackened. (I presumed from being so old.) There were some receipts for dues paid to his union, and a Baptismal Certificate, which I later learned was not valid. Also there was eighteen thousand dollars held by the Treasury Department that my father had in a bank account when he died. All of this sat unclaimed at the Treasury Department for twelve years.

The mere thought that my father laid buried for all those years without a headstone was more than I could bear. In October 1998 my sister and I applied to the VA for a headstone. I thought it might make me feel better, but it didn't. The plaque was free and was paid for by the Veterans Administration. Johnnie-Frances and I split the cost of the installation. I believe she actually did it for me and not our father. In that moment this was okay with me.

All of the hopes I had ever had of gazing

into my father's eyes, celebrating our birthdays, catching up after the first three years of my life, touching his cheek, kissing his forehead, whispering I love you, or learning about his side of my family all disappeared in that very moment. I was devastated.

I later read my sister's letters over and over and came across the one that said I should send her the original documents from the county, and perhaps later she would pass them on to me. I had forgotten about her suggestions on what to do when I received the package, or perhaps it simply went in one ear and out of the other. I was not about to separate from the only original personal papers that were available from our father that was in his possession before his death. I sent her copies.

She had only been living in Kansas City for a few months and was very unhappy with her house arrangements due to mold and mildew in the basement; she started searching for another place to live. I volunteered to go and help her move. She was definitely reluctant to have our first meeting on a nerve-racking situation such as moving. I insisted because by now I knew her "no" meant "yes." Besides, who wouldn't want or need some help. She had a lot of stuff. It would be the first time we laid eyes on each other. Nothing quite so exhilarating had ever happened to me. I was forty-three and she was fifty-three. Anyway, I was dying to meet her and wanted it to happen sooner than later.

I had a small, older travel trailer for several years. At certain times, it felt like home to me. I packed what I needed for a couple of months and was on my way to Kansas City. In my opinion, we initially were both very happy to find each other. From the pictures we exchanged, we definitely looked like we were related.

I was in the middle of nowhere and found a grocery store with a spacious parking lot. I assumed it would be a safe haven. I had been sleeping for several hours when I awoke to some music. I looked out of the side trailer window and, to my surprise, there were about seventy-five people doing line dancing. That was the last thing I expected. I was trapped in the parking lot, so I slept to my heart's content. When I later woke up, the parking lot was vacant, and I was on my merry way.

My sister was dealing with many issues in her life, and her mother was not in good health. We were similar in some ways, but different in others. She was still a nurse, but I had become holistic. This turned out to be quite a clash. I won't even get into her mother and my foster mother's similar personalities. After two years of getting to know each other, we went separate ways. My story is not really about her, but it was an interesting part of my journey and very enlightening.

Chapter Seven
Snoballs in the Desert

It was about this time I was getting burned out with the snoball business. I was entertaining the idea of becoming a massage therapist. I had been involved in natural healing about ten years and felt like I had substantial healing occurring within. If this had not been the case, I would not have had the ability to attempt to be this studious.

I enrolled in one of the most unique schools in the country. Little did I realize that the Southwest Institute of Healing Arts would change my life a bit more. Two hundred hours and five months later it became clear that taking herbs certainly helped me regain my memory. This was a big improvement from high school. I was indeed a licensed massage therapist in the State of Arizona.

At the time of my father's death, he was a resident of Winterhaven, California. He was transported to a bigger hospital specializing in head trauma in Phoenix. Consequently, he had to remain there and was buried in a Phoenix cemetery. I didn't know a corpse was not allowed to be transported across state lines without special arrangements. I decided I wanted to visit the place where he last resided. I packed up my travel trailer and headed to Yuma, which is just across the little bridge to Winterhaven. It was at the juncture of Mexico, Arizona, and California. As I arrived, it seemed like a horrible place to breathe, much less live. Now I'm glad it all happened before I really began to know and love my father. I would have had a lot more

grief and regrets. I hated Winterhaven.

1915-1987

He lived meagerly in an older trailer at an Indian reservation trailer park, which ten years later would be next door to the casino. Unbelievably, there were a couple of ladies that knew my father. One lady said the week before the suicide he spoke about killing himself. She told him God would not approve and he would not go to heaven. One of the ladies said, earlier that day before the gunshot incident my father was at her gate yelling for her to come out, but she was on a long distance telephone call. That was the last time she saw him alive. I didn't speak to the other lady, but I received a short letter from her daughter. Her parents were elderly and lived right next door. She said they could hear him talking to himself before they heard two gunshots. They called 911 when they found my father lying on the ground under a tree.

The week before my father's death he told his neighbors he had a daughter, but he didn't know where she was. Until my father's dying day, he never told anyone he had a second daughter – the daughter who would always regret not being able to be there for him. The thought that my father died alone absolutely breaks my heart. I don't think that will ever change. I didn't realize how I would come to despise the Fourth of July. My father's last day on this earth was July 3, 1987.

One of the ladies said my father had an accent. That, coupled with the fact that my biological father would disappear for weeks at a time for work when I was three years old, would explain why I had a fascination with Uncle Burke's absence, accent, and the confusion in my little mind forty years prior. Not only had I missed him but I also had never forgotten my father's unusual accent and tone and the connection I had with him.

Not long after the end of the relationship between my sister and me and the completion of my massage training, I was beginning to experience a very uncomfortable feeling in my inner thigh area. At first I thought perhaps I was straining too much while doing Chi Quong. More pain and five months later I realized I had Lyme disease. The sensation would go from my thigh to my knee. Once I diagnosed myself and ordered the specific herbs to address this horrible dis-ease, I was without pain in three days and back to normal in no time.

The Lyme disease made me crazy and out of

control to the point of selling my house and moving back to Louisiana. I returned to Jeanerette. I rented a beautiful hundred-year-old house with an octagon-windowed room in the front. I later realized the lady who rented the house to me was many years prior one of my customers when I shelled peas for Pa.

I called my old friend Christin to tell her the news that I was back. She came over with her husband Joe, and they helped me unload my packed twenty-four-foot U-Haul truck. It was nice reconnecting with old friends. It was even nicer to have help unloading my worldly possessions. By this time Christin had two sons in their twenties.

I would drive the hundred and twenty miles to New Orleans every weekend to work doing massage. When I left my lovely home, I felt fine. When I returned during the week, I was not feeling so well. And so it was.

As with most Victorian houses, it had a wonderful veranda. It seemed like the ceiling was over fifteen feet high. There was a huge double drawing room door that separated the living room from the dining room. I had never lived in a place that had a foyer, but it definitely spoke volumes for this Victorian treasure. After fifteen months of living there, I realized why I was sick all the time. I couldn't have guessed that beneath the stately wooden floors there was a killer mold silently attacking me daily.

Learning about my daddy was new to me and didn't bother me so much initially. But with each month that passed by, it got a little more difficult. I acquired a computer and was introduced to the world of the Internet. Little did I know that this would open doors as never before.

I arrived in my old stomping grounds, Jeanerette, with a nice chunk of cash from the profit earned on selling my house in Phoenix. I made it a point to find that old boyfriend whose graduation ring I had lost twenty-seven years before. As I pulled up to his driveway, I was nervous. I honked the horn because there was an eight-foot chain link fence surrounding his property which was, to say the least, a little weird. As this man came out, I tried to find the boy in the face of this man who was approaching me. I said, "Andy," and he said, "Yes," so I assumed I had the right person. I asked, "Do you have your graduation ring?" He said, "No, I lost it." I said, "You didn't lose it, I did." I was surprised when he called me by my name. He was surprised as well that I was standing there. I handed him an envelope with one hundred dollars in it. He said, "You don't have to do this." Smiling as I left, I felt great relief after all those years.

It had only been twenty-six years since I lived there. All of my old friends were married, had moved away, or had died. I did manage to briefly connect with a couple of old boyfriends. It didn't matter if I could only make contact with them for an hour or so.

After so many years I reconnected with Kevin. I asked him about the time I was trying to get out of the water and split my pants. He said he only saw my blue floral underwear. I had to laugh.

Then I found this little bar that was located on Main Street as you were leaving the little town of New Iberia, west of Jeanerette and on the way to Lafayette. There was a band whose music was labeled as "Swamp Pop." Out of the blue, this band would advertise a concert just two days prior to a particular night. Word gets around fast in little towns.

My favorite song was "Mardi Gras Mambo." I didn't have a guy to dance with, so I danced with my bar stool and loved it. I met a few new people and a couple of people I had known before. One night I got so drunk that if I hadn't closed one eye to drive home, I don't think I would have arrived alive. There was never a close call, but I never did that again.

I took pleasure in calling my mother to gloat about finding out about my father, his daughter, and my half-sister. I wanted to rub it in her face because I hadn't talked to her in about fifteen years. She couldn't be bothered with trying to help me find my father. She couldn't have cared less, which was heartbreaking for me. She seemed to have a knack for making me feel less than special.

I decided to move back to Phoenix. It had only been two years since I had found my father, and it was beginning to permeate my soul. It wasn't until I returned to Phoenix that I started having a desire to have my birthright. And what is a birthright? It's the right to have both your mother's and your father's names on the piece of paper, a birth certificate, which is issued at the time of your birth. If that is the definition, I was forty-six years old and didn't have my birthright yet. It was at this point that I changed my name to Rose.

I chose to reside in a senior citizen RV park twenty-five miles north of Phoenix at the beginning of the desert leaving the city, at the one thousand foot altitudes. I bought the cutest little one bedroom trailer I'd ever seen. It was the newest trailers available and was called Park Models by Cavco. It had cathedral ceilings, ceiling fans, Berber carpets, and a lot of storage space. I choose the color schemes. I could live with everything blue in my life, as it was still my favorite color. It was a very serene place. The entire front of the trailer was comprised of three glass windows, so the view was fantastic. There were mountains in the background and a lake beyond the mountains. The sunsets were phenomenal, the rain storms outrageous, and the wildlife was wild. There were wild pigs called javelinas that ran around in packs every night. Coyotes were also abundant. They made their presence obvious with their hollering. Every once in a while I would see a snake. Once, I saw a skunk chasing a snake.

There was an older man called Tonee who lived a few spaces away from mine who befriended me from the moment I moved in. He was a loud-mouth man who grew up in New York and settled in the RV park years before with his wife, who by this time had died. He was alone and I was alone. Later, he told me, he knew that some of the long-time tenants would stab me in the back. Sure enough, there was a woman who lived behind me who was always complaining about something I was doing wrong.

I enjoyed the many evenings that I went to Tonee's to chat for hours at a time. He was overweight and old, so I helped him work on his car. He was one of only a very few men in my adult life who didn't hit on me. If there was a car part to replace which could only be reached by going under the car, I did the deed. He was grateful to have a friend and so was I.

Tonee went to garage sales on Fridays and Saturdays. On Sundays he would rent a table at a swap meet and sell whatever he bought in the days before. I had to get rid of a lot of my stuff that didn't fit into my trailer, so I went with him as soon as I moved into my new trailer. He even volunteered to put up an awning for me to park my car under. I could never have afforded to have it done. We got the entire carport erected in two days.

I used to grill all the time. I cooked for the entire week. Tonee didn't have many teeth and couldn't eat the meat, but I would always make sure to add yams or sweet potatoes for him.

Tonee even loaned me two thousand dollars once so I could pay for the annual rental space. I paid him back within a couple of months. It was nice to have that kind of credit and someone that trusted me enough to help.

Soon after, I started working and had to drive four or five days a week south on I-17 to downtown Phoenix. I was working through the concierge at a huge four-star hotel chain in downtown Phoenix. Having to pass by the exit street sign which led to the cemetery where my father was buried started to make me mentally ill. There was no escaping that pain. It was just a reminder of how dishonorably my father was put to rest. I was forced to relive the fact over and over again that, in my opinion, my father had been buried in a manner no better than a dog. He never had a prayer, a flower, a visitor, or a thought; and what about dignity, honor, and integrity.

There wasn't a day that went by that I didn't cry. I couldn't get the fact out of my head that this man, my father, had been there for ten years while hundreds of people walked over his grave never knowing he put his life on the line and fought for their freedom. It bothered me more than anything ever had in my entire life.

A couple of years went by. In June 2003 I googled my father's name and up popped his photo from fifty years prior. Little did I know that the 10th Mountain Division Resource Center was created at the Denver Library to memorialize the 10th Mountain Division. My father was in the 85th Regiment, Co K and the Headquarters Division in the 10th Mountain. The photo taken June 5, 1944, of Co K consisted of one hundred and thirty-one men comprising three battalions (see Appendix). My dad was in the third battalion. I had no idea that this very photo might help me win my own war. My father is almost in the exact middle of the photo. Looking at the picture, he is the man to the left of the gentleman with the hand on his left shoulder.

(Copyright by the Denver Public Library, 10th Mountain Division Collection)

It had been perhaps four years since I'd spoken to my half-sister. I decided to send her a picture of my father since he was allegedly her father as well. After calculating the timeframe of the photo, it became clear that it was taken within two weeks of Johnnie-Frances' conception, if he was indeed her father. By this time I knew for a fact that just because a man's name is on a birth certificate does not mean he is the biological father.

I began a crusade to have my father's remains transferred to a veterans' cemetery. Once again, my intentions would go nowhere fast. I had no rights to my father. I started with the most logical of possibilities. I sent e-mails to a couple of attorneys but to no avail. The Veterans Administration had done all they could do, which was to put a headstone at his grave, even if the grave was in the wrong cemetery. There was a very compassionate veteran representative that listened to my sob story, but that was all he could do. Typically, it ended up being a huge crying session for me.

How was I going to prove I was the daughter of this man who had been dead for eighteen years? It would take a month and a bottle of brandy to compose a new letter to each and every person to whom I could plead for help. Among those attempts were letters sent to President George Bush, his father, and the Governor of California, because my father was a resident of that state even though he was buried in Arizona. I couldn't believe I actually got a response from the Governor of California. When I read the letter, it didn't even sound like "We feel for you, but we can't help you." It felt like "Why don't you just slit your throat." I even went to the popular wartime Senator of Arizona's office to no avail.

I also wrote to the Governor of Arizona. In my letter, I explained my dilemma. I poured my guts out, saying some days I didn't want to live. I was not about to kill myself, but it felt like that would be the better of two evils. They naturally chose to read between the lines and not what I was saying specifically. As a result, they actually sent a deputy over to spy on me. I guess they had to verify their hunches. I didn't get any sympathy or help, and it pissed me off to be patronized.

As usual I took several trips back and forth to New Orleans every year. It was Jazz Festival 2004, and I was invited to the family reunion of my oldest dear friend Rosa. Her mom and dad, all her sisters, and her brother were there. I'd known them for over forty years. The subject of my third grade teacher came up. I asked if I was the only one who thought that she was the meanest person on the face of the earth. They agreed Mrs. Stevens was notoriously mean. I was informed that she was now an attorney.

Mrs. Stevens had expelled me in third grade.

I didn't bring a gun to school, nor did I steal anything. My problem was I didn't know when or how to shut up. I was a kid and devastated by my real mother deserting me. Being abused by my foster mom didn't help either. Since this world was becoming more conscious, I started fantasizing that she might now realize that I had a legitimate reason for my disruptive personality. I called her, thinking she might have become a little bit compassionate in the last thirty-five years. I had an appointment with the lady who made such a lasting impression on me so many years ago. I was not at all surprised that she was now an attorney – one that was similar to a shark.

As we sat face-to-face so many years later, I could tell she hadn't change at all. I told her the truth about the abuse and my dilemma, but she was as cold as ice or maybe worse. She had the nerve to say maybe I needed that in my life. I looked at her in her wheel chair (due to a stroke) and wanted to say maybe she deserved that throne she's on, and maybe she deserved someone wiping her butt ten times a day, but I didn't have the heart or nerve to give her a dose of her own medicine.

A few weeks later her office advised me that

she would not be able to assist me because she was dealing with another issue related to her health. It was this very teacher who would give me hope and a new road to travel. She suggested going to court and trying to have my birth certificate amended. In all my years of efforts, this was the first time I'd heard of this procedure. Once again, I didn't have the money to hire a lawyer to attempt to accomplish this. I returned to my home in Phoenix and started researching attorneys. The more I got rejected and denied, the more I tried, cried, and drank.

At this point I started thinking about my mother again and decided she was the only mother I had, so I decided to call her and attempt a reconciliation. As usual she was receptive. I asked her to please try to remember something about my father. She managed to come up with a few incidents, all of which occurred before I was three years old. She also held the key to the opportunity of obtaining my birthright. I thought that was the least she could do. She said my biological father would twist my already curly auburn hair around a pencil as I sat on his lap.

My favorite incident was probably the first. My biological father came over one day and was telling my mother he didn't think I knew if I was a boy or a girl. She told him to ask me. So, he said to me, "Come here my little boy." I responded with my hand on my little hip, "I not a boy, I a girl." He asked, "How do you know you're a girl?" and I responded, "My mommy told me." He called me Lovey and I would say, "You Yuvey Yuvey." I will never forget that.

There was another incident when we were returning home one evening, and he was going to put the key in the keyhole to open it. I started screaming and crying. I wanted to open the door, so he gave me the collection of keys. Of course, I was unable to open the door, so I handed him the keys and said "Opey the dopey, Yuvey Yuvey."

My mother would have me believe my father didn't want to have anything to do with me. She cannot comprehend that my father fought on the front lines. She would say, "I can't understand why you care so much about your father. He didn't care about you." My father was from the Old World where a man was a man and brought home the bacon, and the woman took care of the kids and the home. He asked her to marry him and for us to be a family in 1968. At that time, the only thing on

Ellie's mind was what was good for Ellie. She was not going to marry any man. When she left West Virginia, she had a man trapped in her body; she was into women. She was a confirmed lesbian and not interested in men any longer. I remember being confused about her man's haircut and wearing men's clothes.

I was born in the last week of December 1955. Now, my mother was telling me that my biological father did not see me until January of 1956. I began to think about that not-so-personalized license plate which was inscribed LYN-056. I couldn't help but wonder if this was coincidental or not.

Another incident with my father happened about a week before Thanksgiving a couple of years later. My father showed up at our house with a turkey. He told my mother never to say a word, but the lady who owned the restaurant on the first floor below our apartment left her door unlocked, and he went in and raided her freezer and took her turkey. Even today I wish I could find that lady and repay her for the turkey. I wonder if my daddy didn't just tell my mother that. Maybe he didn't actually steal the turkey; just maybe he bought it but didn't want my mother to know. Either way it makes me smile just to know something about my father. Another tidbit was that my father used his teabag twice. I thought everyone did, since I did too.

My mother also mentioned my biological father had a wooden rocking chair made especially for me when my little brother was born because I couldn't fit in the ones at the store. I wanted to be able to rock my new baby brother. Thus my request to Santa when I was four years old was for a "wocking chair" and Peanut the Chihuahua. My mother thought the name was Peewee.

The Internet was changing my life. I couldn't help but wonder about my mother's first son. There was a website that let you search for birth dates of missing people. I asked my mother if she'd ever thought about him, but it didn't seem to interest her. I had never given much thought to him either and quickly abandoned the idea.

My mother told me at fourteen years old she was raped by her mother's sister's husband. Perhaps it was that experience that would never allow her to be the best mother she could be. Her mantra was, she did the best she could. She always claimed to love me; however, I never felt the love, ever. Perhaps it was also her guilt with the absence of her first-born which prevented her from even being a decent mother. I would never have the opportunity to learn about my mother or her ways. I tried to excuse my mother's inability to show her motherly love, but there came a point for me to stop letting her treat me like a stepchild.

The war with Iraq started around May 1, 2003. Until this point I only heard, read, and imagined how difficult war was on the men who fight for their country. By this time I was actually watching the reality of the war on the television. I would cry just imagining the tragedy of it all. It had been several years of tracing my father's footsteps for his time fighting for our freedoms. I couldn't help but think of my own father's hardships.

I decided to call my father's so-called nephew who lived just north of Jupiter, Florida. I asked him to help me get my father's eighteen thousand dollars which he left behind and the Treasury Department was holding for eighteen years. I confided in him about my path and pain in looking for my father and fighting for my father's dignity. He confided in me about his father, allegedly my father's brother. He was quick to tell me that his father was brash, loud, and rude. I had already experienced his rudeness years before when he hung up on me. One would think he was different than his father.

I didn't have rights to my father and couldn't imagine how I was going to accomplish the task without his help. Why should Imperial County have my father's money indefinitely? This nephew didn't even know my father or that he died or where he was buried. He agreed to help me, so I made arrangements to send him a letter to use with all my father's information. All he had to do was sign and mail the letter.

Some of my closest friends were tired and bored hearing me cry about my father. Bubby approached me with the idea that his friend from college who was an attorney was going to help me go to court. It didn't take me long to get back to New Orleans. My "dream team" consisted of a real estate attorney and a notary. My attorney warned and prepared me for the worst, and I accepted the fact that the chances were slim, but that didn't scare me in the least. Rejection was just another part of life. It didn't stop me from being extremely nervous as we headed to the courthouse on October 29, 2004. The notary was able to get us through the door. We spent six hours running around the courthouse. We had to go to the District Attorney's office for my background check. It would be the most important and ultimately the most nerve-racking day of my life. It even topped my wedding day.

Little did I know that one year, four months, and nine days later that photo taken before D-Day of my father's unit would play a major role in my getting my birthright. As we stood before the Honorable Judge M. Landrieu, my mind was racing so fast I thought my heart would pound right out of my body or that my legs would buckle. Everything depended on my ten minutes in front of the judge. I was ready, as ready as I could be. Fortunately, my mother's husband and the man who had been listed as the father on my birth certificate were still alive, and I was able to get affidavits from both of them stating they didn't have sex for two years before I was born. You would think that over the last forty years it would occur to him that I was not his daughter, but that didn't happen. I was grateful for the cooperation of both of them.

My lawyer spoke first. The passion was not there, and I could feel myself sinking and losing faith. I was praying to God with all my might for some type of help from a "higher power." At this point I whipped out my daddy's army photo and began to cry even more. I believe the most important statement of all was that my daddy fought on the front lines for our freedom. He deserved to be buried honorably.

When it was time for the judge to make her decision, all I could hear was "ROSE I DO NOT WANT TO DO THIS," and then she said, "BUT I AM." I could hardly hear her through my tears. Then she said, "I DON'T KNOW IF THIS WILL HELP." For the very first time in twenty-two years I did not get rejected. I heard it but could hardly believe it. It was so overwhelming that it would take two months for it to penetrate and permeate my mind, and for me to fully understand what it meant. I was elated, but I think my body was in shock to the tenth degree. It meant that I now had rights to my father and to be my father's daughter. It didn't matter that I was a daughter to a dead corpse. I couldn't help but think about the judge saying, "I don't want to do this." My mother had lied on my birth certificate; there was no proof she was not lying on the affidavit that I provided for my

"Court Order." I couldn't help but believe there actually was a "higher power" assisting me. Whatever it was, I welcomed it without any questions.

While my plan was in motion to get my father's money, that nephew in Florida had already stolen it from me. I would have never asked that lying thief to help me if I had had the inclination to wait a couple of months more to obtain the rights to my father. It wasn't about the money. The money was coincidental. I had been working on this quest to find and honor my father eighteen years, and there simply happened to be eighteen thousand dollars involved. It was as if that money was waiting for me. Everything I had worked on for eighteen years was destroyed by him in eighteen minutes. He had recently inherited money from his own father. In order to move on, I thought, "I couldn't lose something I never had."

It wasn't long before I realized my real mother hadn't changed one bit. As always, it was all about her. I was telling her about my accomplishments with the snoball business when she said, "I always wanted you kids to do good things." It was like she was talking to someone else. I just wanted her to say, I always wanted "You" to do good, not you kids. I was hurt and furious and said, "You kids!" I slammed the phone down. I had finally had enough and realized that I would never try to reconcile with my mother ever again.

As a kid I remember her two favorite mantras: (1) "Kids are to be seen and not heard" and (2) "Do as I say, not as I do." I was not about to try to explain anything to her, but I was determined to make her a thing of the past again.

Approximately two months after my court order I was still in shock. Senator Bob Dole was a member of the 10th Mountain Division, 86th Regiment Co. I. I e-mailed his public relations secretary and asked what I should do now. She responded that my court order would get the process started. And, so it would.

Chapter Eight
My Dream Comes True or My Worst
Nightmare

My first plan of action was to have my father's body exhumed from the cemetery (where anyone's grandmother could be buried) and interred at the Cave Creek National Memorial Cemetery, a veteran's cemetery where he belonged since day one after his death. The funeral home director, the medical examiner, and the Veterans Administration all had to be coordinated. Some of the expenses had to be paid out of my pocket, but the Veterans Administration once again had another headstone engraved. I was very impressed with the fact they didn't oppose. Perhaps they'd been through this process before.

I had intentions of having DNA testing and had the DNA company send a kit. Arrangements were made with the funeral director, who would have to retrieve the bone to be used. It would be my only opportunity to have a DNA test done. Typically, a DNA test costs about three to five hundred dollars and can be done in less than a week. The DNA test on my father took a month and costs almost fifteen hundred dollars. It was the longest month of my life, but the results came back. I was my father's daughter. They returned the bones of my father to me, and I carried them around for a while in a plastic baggie before having them cremated. They will remain in my possession until death do us part.

From this point on when I came across anything that had to do with my father, I had the right to request whatever it was. This is when, where, and how five sentences about my father turned into fifteen pounds of research papers, all having to do with him. It was official. I was this dead man's daughter.

The first personal information I received from the county where my father lived at the time of his death included some receipts from his Boilermaker-Blacksmith National Brotherhood Association dues. Between January and March 2005, I wrote to the Association for any information having to do with my father. I received a list of the companies with which my father was employed between 1961 and 1975. It was so liberating to have access to my father's personal and private information.

Shortly thereafter, I was able to go to the original funeral home where records from my father's 1987 burial were located. I vividly remember the day seven years prior when I stopped by to plead with the funeral director to let me have my father's file. He was not cooperative, wouldn't budge, and didn't care that I was crying like a baby. I told him not to lose that file because I would be back. I was true to my word as I was there to collect my father's file seven years later.

I also applied for my father's file at the head trauma hospital where he took his last breath. I was not about to look at the devastating file, but I still wanted possession of it. Eventually, I would look at it.

It took nine months of waiting, but the day I became the recipient of my father's army medals was one of the proudest of my life. There was a Victory medal, a Bronze medal, the Ruptured Duck, and the Infantry medal. The Infantry medal was my favorite because of the beautiful blue border. I cherished these with all my heart. Sometimes I break them out at a 4th of July party in honor of my father. In a way I was extremely grateful that my father had not received his four medals from WWII. On the opposite end of the spectrum, it pained me just as much to know he didn't care about receiving them for himself.

At the end of September 2005, I was on vacation in New Orleans for three weeks. The Friday before Katrina, Bubby had a great "Hurricane Party." We were partying like animals and slamming down Crash and Burns. The hurricane was going towards Florida, but it took a turn overnight. I woke up groggy, and had to cut the vacation short, pack, and evacuate.

My packing plans always involved seven or more hours. I was finally on my way back to the desert. I drove like never before. Finally, Sunday evening I got some news on the radio that New Orleans survived the storm. A half a day later as I arrived in Phoenix, I couldn't believe what I was hearing. New Orleans was eighty percent under water. How could that be? I was grateful to not have gotten this devastating news as I drove seventeen hundred miles across country. It was bad enough I was running from the storm.

The next five weeks I cried like a baby

because I was hearing about friends with difficulties. I was not watching the television, but I could hear it. I recognized the voice as a girlfriend who was crying because her cousin had found her brother dead. The cousin put the body in the front yard in a bathtub, but it was nowhere to be found. There was also the story about my dear friend Mr. Gabriel, who played the coins in the aluminum tray on stage with the pianist at Pat O'Brien's. Mr. Eddie was missing for a long time. Later it was discovered he died in his attic, where he rode out the storm.

A couple of months later I returned to New Orleans. As I got closer to the city, I began to get apprehensive and had a very eerie feeling. All the road signs were all leaning to the north, one after the other. Depression got the best of me, so I pulled the car to the side of the road and cried for thirty minutes for the city I loved so much. I couldn't help but feel the similarity between the pain I felt for this tragedy and the pain I felt as I fought for my father. I thought how the people and the entire city of New Orleans now felt the pain I'd felt all these years as I searched for the man whose blood runs through my veins. I would not have wished this on my worst enemy. It was an unimaginable pain to say the least.

I obtained a medical report on my father from two years before his death. The nurse asked the questions, and she transcribed my father's responses. At that time he was advised of a prostate concern, which he was not at all interested in talking about. He was having an operation for a hemorrhoid. I could imagine my daddy sitting before her. As individual and personal as it was about my father, it sounded like they could have been some of my own responses. He drank very little alcohol, but he did smoke some. Sometimes, running the cold water was the only way he could urinate. In the same report I couldn't help but think about the broken rib mentioned. Did he incur this during the war? I've had several rib injures over the years. He mentioned ringing in his right ear. I also have ringing in my right ear. It made me feel even more like I am my father's daughter. In addition to those similarities, it's wild that we would both migrate to the southwest corner of the United States.

It was the part about him having a prostate problem that gave me some of the answers I think I needed. I would hate to think that on

July 3, 1987, my father was having a bad day and decided to end his life. I honestly believe he perhaps had prostate cancer and suicide was his way out. At seventy-three years of age, my father was not on any kind mediation when he died. I am not on any kind of medication. On the other hand, I would be willing to bet my mother is on a few medications.

It was the first Mardi Gras after Katrina. There was a somber air about the city that I had never experienced before. It was the saddest of sad. My heart ached, but I was determined to have a good time, as was everyone else.

I had been working on my book for some time but knew I needed help in that department. I knew I was not a writer, but I also knew that I had a story to tell. In an effort to move forward with it, I had a brainstorm. I bought a six-foot white plastic banner and was on a mission. I used a large, black chisel marker pen and wrote, "Anderson, please call me." I listed my phone number. It was plain and simple. As he so compassionately covered the weeks and months after Katrina, I thought Anderson Cooper could and would help me. I asked

Bubby if I could lay my banner across the top of the Magic Bus. Bubby rarely if ever said no, so I tied it down. I thought maybe Anderson would be flying overhead in a helicopter, and I wanted an opportunity to attract his attention.

Within thirty minutes, some friends arrived at the Magic Bus and asked if I wanted to go walking down Royal Street. We started walking, and I told them about my banner. When we turned onto Royal Street, one of them said, "Look, there's Anderson Cooper." I was freaked out and started running towards him screaming "Anderson, Anderson." There I was out of breath, staring him in the eyes. I told him I had a great story. I only thought I was prepared, but I wasn't. I couldn't find a piece of paper to give him my phone number, so my friend gave me his business card, and I jotted down my phone number on the back. I asked him to please call me, but I never heard from him.

A couple of months after Mardi Gras, I found myself without a dog again. This time I was going to purchase the dog my biological father wanted me to have when I was four years old. I went to a breeder just over the Louisiana border in Mississippi. She had several Chihuahuas for five or six hundred dollars. I didn't have that much to spend, so she showed me a little black brindle female without a tail from birth. No one else wanted her, but I fell in love with her instantly. Lovey would be the next love of my life.

I had always had a dog that weighed at least twenty-five pounds. For the first three or four months, she was less than three pounds. I didn't realize how such a small dog would alter my life. I had to change many of the ways I did things. I had to slow down and pay more attention to the floor or the ground. One wrong move could have ended everything. I didn't realize she would have to use the potty every hour and eat eight times a day. I was so in love with her it didn't matter.

Lovey is so her grandfather's granddaughter. She seems to think she has the 10th Mountain in her. When a large dog goes by her gate in the front yard, she wants to go at it. She's barking with diligence and her spine hair is at attention. On the other hand, when the wind blows through the palm tree, it scares her to death. I tell her, "The tree's going to get you," and she runs to me.

When I drink an alcoholic beverage, it is usually brandy, gin and tonic with lime, or

Merlot wine. Of course, Lovey is right at my side looking like she wants a taste. Every once in a while, I let her indulge in a drop. I'll dip my finger in my drink, and, yes, she licks it off my finger, wanting more. Then I think, You are your mother's daughter, too.

I've heard that we all dream; however, I rarely remember anything about my nightly dreams. Occasionally, I remember a little but nothing that makes much sense. Usually, it's something crazy or silly. Literally for ten years, since 1997 when I first found my father at the cemetery, I'd been praying, wishing, hoping, and begging for my father to come to me in my dreams. I had invested so many tears, a lot of years, energy, and efforts, and for what? I would never have been thanked, rewarded, or acknowledged, not that it's what I expected. I just wanted my father to know how much I loved him. Once again I had surrendered any ideas of my father, and Bam, the gates opened.

Finally, the day arrived. It was a date I will never forget: October 5, 2008. The body of the man and a vague memory of the face that I barely could remember (since the last time I saw him I was only four years old) was looking into my eyes like forty-nine years before. No names were mentioned. He knew who I was, and I knew who he was. It wasn't like a dream but more like a personal visitation in my sleep. It was a direct conversation. I cannot say it was a voice. It seemed and sounded like words were spoken, but perhaps it was only feelings. It was as if someone came to my house and knocked on the door and was face-to-face with me.

I only had two photographs of my father. One in which he was twenty-nine years old and he wore a green garrison cap which showed no hair, and the other in which he was sixty years old and almost bald with a little hair around the back and the sides. He didn't look like either picture. He looked to be approximately forty years old. It was like a short perm with perfect salt and pepper curls.

My first words to him were, "I've missed you so much." He responded, "I came as soon as I knew you were looking for me." I don't remember thinking it had been forty-nine years. He had a lady with him. I asked, "Is that your wife or girlfriend?" and he simply said, "No." I left it at that. It was the feelings I had that excited me. He left a time or two. I would say, "Are you coming back?"and he would say, "Yes." And he did. I had the feeling that he was going to sleep, eat, or shower. I suppose I didn't know what else to think. I guess I just wanted him to come back. I cannot remember any conversation when he came back. I had never experienced anything like this.

The funeral director also said that when they took the cement cover off the coffin, my dad had his shirt, pants, and socks intact, but when they touched the coffin, everything disintegrated. In a way I wished I had seen it for myself. On the other hand, I'm grateful to be spared the pain and lasting memory of my dead father's body. He also said my father had long curly hair, which was validating.

It was the first time in a year I actually slept eight hours uninterrupted. I had gone to sleep around 2 am and woke up at 10 am absolutely freaked out. This was the pinnacle of excitement in my life. I thought about the visit, and for a brief moment wondered why I didn't ask this or that, but quickly decided none of it mattered. What mattered was I felt loved by my father. I was already relishing the idea of the next visitation.

I know my father is buried in Phoenix, but I would have thought that he would have come to me in my sleep while I was in New Orleans.

Within a week I decided to leave Phoenix and head to New Orleans, where we were last physically together in 1959. I wanted more warm, fuzzy feelings.

In 2011, I revisited the 10th Mountain Division Descendants Association. Since June 2003, I had been in receipt of the June 6, 1944, group photo from which the photo of my father was extracted. I started focusing on the group. Mr. Rios, the President of the 10th Mountain Division Descendants Association at the time, gave me a roster with phone numbers and addresses of the living veterans who were in the photo with my father. I so wished I hadn't waited so many years to follow up on this.

Surprisingly, there were sixteen possibilities. These men are now between eighty-three and ninety-three years old. Several men had died, a couple of phone numbers were no longer in service, a couple didn't remember anything, a few just remembered my father's face when they looked at his picture, and a couple couldn't hear or understand what I was asking or talking about. I got to speak to a widower who was the wife of one of the gentlemen standing exactly to the right of my father. Lieutenant Hauptman remembered he was about five years older than the other men, but didn't know anything personal. I have plans to visit Mr. Hauptman in Billings, Montana, in the very near future. He must be about ninety years old. Each and every man I contacted, and a couple of their wives, could not have been more pleasant and sympathetic. I could tell they wished they had some news for me. I do believe this was my father's only family. It would have been nice to learn something new about my father, but it was an honor and a privilege as well as amazing to talk to these men who were standing in a photo with my father sixty-seven years ago.

As I waited for a year with anticipation for the day I would leave to visit Mr. Hauptman, I was excited and looked forward to the journey. I would finally be face-to-face with the last known gentleman that gave my father orders in the army in 1944. He wasn't the lieutenant of my father's platoon, but at one time he did give my father orders to help clear bodies after a day of war. He definitely didn't have a clue how much he meant to me.

The week prior to leaving there was an unexpected snowstorm that pummeled Casper, Wyoming, a town that I would be traveling through. I was on pins and needles, with fear of being in the middle of a snowstorm; it was something very unfamiliar to me.

Not to mention that I had a time constraint, since Mr. Hauptman had plans to go on his annual elk hunting trip with his family and friends. In my opinion, the first couple of days of my travels were perfect. It was cloudy all day, and I enjoyed the different landscapes, though I couldn't adequately describe a single scene. One thing was certain: I had to get there, and fast.

I left on Tuesday, planning to meet him that Friday. I arrived in Billings Thursday night. As I drove into the town on Interstate 90, it was amazing and grand, and the temperature was crisp and cold. I over-looked the illuminated city, finding myself filling with a majestic feeling that it was just for me.

At about 9 pm I phoned Mr. Hauptman to let him know I had arrived. He gave me directions to his house. He suggested the Dude Ranch, which I misconstrued as Nude Ranch. After checking out the rate for the night, I decided to sleep in my car in a safe-looking neighborhood only a few miles from his home. That would pay for two tanks of gas. I could hardly wait for the next morning.

I decided not to tell him about sleeping in my car.

Waking up early and heading west on the main street, I entered his subdivision along the side of the *Rimrocks*, or *the Rims*, and encountered a very strange event.

What looked like four turkeys perfectly aligned themselves across the entire width of the street in front of me, as though they were in drill formation. I had to get into the left lane and go around them to proceed forward. In that moment I made a mental note to ask him if they were indeed turkeys or perhaps only roadrunners, because they were not the big, hefty featherless turkeys that I had witnessed around Thanksgiving. I was excited as could be.

Knocking on his door at 9 am, I didn't quite know what to expect. I only had the photo from sixty years ago. As he opened the door, I immediately recognized his face. At this point, the last thing on my mind was the turkeys; they were gone with the wind.

He lead me to his media room, where there were a few chairs, a television, and a few shelving units which displayed his Army memorabilia and, most importantly, his 10th Mountain Division books, magazines, tapes, and DVDs. There was a beautiful view of the woods behind his property. He said that at various times during the year, mule deer and other wildlife basked in his unfenced backyard.

I was in heaven and in awe to be in his presence. He was very tall (about 6 foot), stocky, and he reminded me of a mountain man, but he had a very hospitable and gentle personality. I'm sure he'd entertained many of his Army friends in that room. He seemed so proud of his history – and so he should be.

Time was flying and it was already time for lunch. Mr. Hauptman invited me to a lunch with him. As we left, Mr. Hauptman got the chance to see the vinyl signs I had on the doors of my Honda Civic. In white five-inch scroll fancy font there was written "The 10th Mountain In Me @kindle," which has been changed to "Rose's War."

Mr. Hauptman said I could choose the restaurant, but I asked him to choose. We jumped into his SUV and headed downtown. I was thrilled to spend more time with him, even though we probably didn't have too much in common; but we talked a lot. He was already my idol. He ordered a Caesar salad and a bowl of chowder. Looking at the menu, my eyes zeroed in on the crab cakes with a light ginger sauce. He agreed it was an excellent choice, which I must say was fabulous. The medallions were small but thick and had a lot of seasonings, which surprised me. They were fried to a golden brown and were nestled on each other. I could have eaten a few more, and more sauce would have been excellent.

When we returned to his home, I moved from the chair to the floor in front of the shelf of books. I wanted to examine whatever he wanted to share with me. There were several books that I recognized because I also had a few familiar books in my collection of the 10th Mountain Division.

I then went out to my car to retrieve my father's file, which had been a work in progress for over fifteen years. I had recently made new files and had everything organized. Actually, it was my pride and joy – it was my life.

In my bag was also a very important memento of some type of yearbook from the 1940s of the 10th Mountain. It contained Army photos of various men and had been owned by another gentleman in that notorious 1944 group photo of the 85th Regiment. After he died, his wife, Ms. Ethel, began her cleaning-out process and sent me the book.

Although Mr. Hauptman didn't own the yearbook, he immediately recognized it. I felt privileged to present it to him. He knew several of the men that were featured in the photos. I was thrilled that he graciously and eagerly accepted it.

It was 3 pm and I had been with Mr. Hauptman non-stop for six hours. It was time to leave, even though I could have stayed there for days. For ninety years old Mr. Hauptman was going strong but needed to prepare for his trip. We exited through his basement, which led to the garage. He bent over a shelf and pulled out about twelve old license plates that were all personalized "10TH MTN." They were all from previous years. When he told me to take a couple of plates, I felt honored and privileged, but I only took one from 2000. He couldn't throw them away and I couldn't refuse the opportunity.

I felt melancholy and headed to Phoenix. Unfortunately, the darkness came too soon, and I missed a lot of the visual beauty of the landscape, but I could feel an energy in the mountains. I had warm, fuzzy feelings.

It wasn't until the very last day of my thirty-three day trip from New Orleans to Billings to Phoenix and back to New Orleans that a lady from New Jersey, who married a guy and now lived in Dallas, acknowledged my book title on my car. I was pulled over in the parking lot of Lowe's fifty miles north of Dallas, eating a sausage biscuit and having a cup of coffee at 6 am. This lady was sitting in her truck, waiting for the store to open. There were approximately eight empty-car spaces that separated us. She started walking towards me and asked if my sign was about the 10th Mountain Division and I said, "Yes." She went on to say how the current 10th Mountain Division had recently been recognized in the Northeast for doing something commendable.

When I returned home and had time to talk to Ms. Ethel, I asked her about the wear and tear of the yearbook, and she said Mr. Martin looked at it a lot.

My only regret about the trip was not knowing about the turkeys. I later called Mr. Hauptman to thank him for such a warm reception during my visit and to ask him about the turkeys. He said they are a part of the neighborhood and have been there for many years, coming and going at will. It's no wonder they stay nice and trim; they are constantly patrolling the area.

The next chapter was graciously gifted to me from Mr. Dennis Hagen, the current archivist for the 10th Mountain Division Resource Center within the Denver Public Library. I don't think Mr. Hagen or the 10th Mountain Division Descendant's Association and members can begin to know how they have contributed to my continuing efforts to find myself, to obtain a little peace within my own war, and to stay connected to my father. It's a wonderful tribute to these heroes you never knew.

Chapter Nine
Brief History of the 10th Mountain Division
Resource Center

In 1984, World War II 10th Mountain Division veteran, Ben Duke (86-L), suggested to staff of the Denver Public Library's Western History Department, that a permanent repository was needed to collect and preserve WWII 10th Mountain Division material. Duke, a member of the board of directors of Vail Associates, a Colorado Ski Hall of Fame inductee, former CEO of Gates Corporation, and Trustee of the Colorado Historical Foundation, was determined to keep the memory of the 10th Mountain Division alive. Almost immediately papers, maps, newspapers and photos began arriving. Shortly thereafter individuals began offering the library items such as skis, parkas, boots and related mountaineering equipment. It became clear that these items could not be kept in a library setting. Wellington Webb, Denver Mayor from 1990-2002, and in 1984 the Chairman of the Denver Public Library Friend's Foundation, wrote a letter to the president of the Colorado Historical Society proposing that the two institutions join together in taking responsibility for 10th Mountain Division materials. The library would be responsible for personal papers and correspondence, photographs, maps, books and other manuscript materials appropriate in a library. The Colorado Historical Society would accept and care for equipment, uniforms and similar material culture artifacts. The next step involved a joint meeting of the Rocky Mountain Chapter of the 10th, the Library and the History Museum. Those attending were asked to support these two institutions as the recommended repository for their 10th related historical items. Everyone in attendance enthusiastically supported the joint venture and voted accordingly. The National Association of the 10th also embraced this concept and Ben Duke moved forward on the first draft of a legal agreement between the Denver Public Library, the Colorado Historical Society and the 10th Mountain Division Association. Duke's draft described the types of materials the Resource Center would collect and how those items would be cared for and used for research and exhibits. Having had experience in writing similar agreements, Hugh Evans (85-C) was asked to join the effort. With a considerable amount of input from others, the agreement was signed by representatives from all three institutions, and the 10th Mountain Division Resource Center became a reality on October 14, 1987. In the beginning, staff at both institutions were able to do the work of organizing, cataloging and preserving material as well as making it available for research and exhibit through the resources of the museum and library. However, as the collections continued to grow, it was clear that additional funding for staff and supplies would be needed. Bill Boddington (86-A), then the President of the Tenth Mountain Division Foundation began sending checks in the amount of $4,000 to $5,000 to the Resource Center each year to help with operating expenses. Though some contract archival work was being done on specific collections at DPL, the funding by the Foundation enabled the Library to hire an archivist to work part time processing 10th collections exclusively. This financial support also enabled the Historical Society to purchase and install much needed space saving storage cabinets for the uniforms and equipment of the WWII 10th. Many other projects in support of the 10th collections have been completed over the years through the financial support of the Foundation and National Association. Through it all, the library and museum continue to provide institutional resources for the proper care and use of the collections. Since 1998, a full time employee at the Denver Public Library has worked exclusively with the 10th collection cataloging incoming material, assisting researchers and corresponding with veterans and their families daily. Barbara Walton guided the 10th Mountain Division from its formation in 1987 until her departure from the Denver Public Library in 2003. Debbie Gemar assumed responsibility for the Resource Center from 2003 to 2006. Dennis Hagen has managed the Resource Center since January 1, 2006. When the Resource Center was created, a 10th Mountain Division Resource Center Advisory Committee was also formed. The committee consists of former Presidents of the Association, an appointed Foundation liaison and other 10th veterans. In recent years, 10th descendants have been invited to join. The committee meets with Resource Center staff annually to review activities at both institutions, advise on activities and evaluate financial need. No other military collection of this size and scope, committed solely to the gathering and preservation of materials from a single WWII Army division, exists in the United States. The Resource Center staff is committed to building and maintaining the 10th collection so that the story of this unique military unit, and the post-war achievements of its veterans, can be told for generations to come. As of January 2007, the collection at Denver Public Library consisted of approximately 350 boxes of papers and ephemeral material, and approximately 15,000 photographs. Over the past twenty years, 907 individual donors from among 10th Mountain Division veterans and family members have contributed materials to the collection. The collection continues to grow and researchers from all over the world contact or visit the Denver Public Library looking for information, photos and film for books, magazine articles, movies and documentary television. The museum loans equipment and clothing to other institutions across the country for exhibits every year and is currently planning a permanent exhibit of 10th artifacts at the Colorado History Museum. In addition to the 10th Mountain Division Resource Center, the Denver Public Library maintains the 10th Mountain Division Room, which is located in the Western History/Genealogy department, at the west end of level 5. It was made possible through the support and generosity of Ben and Maud

Duke. Active with the library and the 10th Mountain Division Association, Ben and Maud wanted to establish a room in the new central library (opened in 1995) in honor of the 10th, where material from the collection could be displayed. They also stipulated that the room was to be a workspace for WHG staff, not strictly a memorial to the men of the 10th. Therefore, the 10th Mountain Division Room serves as a projects and meeting room where a variety of items from the 10th archival collection at DPL can be showcased. The public is welcome to visit the 10th Mountain Division Room during regular library hours.

Select Bibliography

Books and Articles:

Benedict, H. Bradley. Ski Troops in the Mud: Kiska Island Recaptured. Published by the author, 1995.
Black, Andy and Charles M. Hampton, The 10th RECON/MTG., Published by the authors 1996.
Brooks, Thomas R., "10th Mountain Division History," in 10th Mountain Division, Turner Publishing Co, Paducah, KY, 1998 (two volumes).

Brooks, Thomas R., and John Imbrie. Mission Udine: The 10th Mountain Division at the Yugoslav Border. Forest Hills, New York: National Association of the 10th Mountain Division, 2005.

Burton, Hal. The Ski Troops. New York: Simon and Schuster, 1971.

Casewit, Curtis W. Mountain Troopers! The Story of the Tenth Mountain Division. New York: Crowell, 1972.

Combat History of the 10th Mountain Division 1944-1945. Fort Benning, Georgia: reprinted from the Infantry School Library, 1977.

Coquoz, Rene L. The Invisible Men on Skis, The Story of the Construction of Camp Hale and the Occupation by the 10th Mountain Division, 1942-1945. Boulder, Colorado: Johnson Publishing Co., 1970.

Dusenbery, Harris. Ski the High Trail. Portland, Oregon: Binford & Mort Publishing, 1991.

Dusenbery, Harris. The North Apennines and Beyond. Portland, Oregon: Binford & Mort Publishing, 1998.

Earle, George F. History of the 87th Mountain Infantry Regiment. United States Army. circa 1945.

Ellis, Robert B. See Naples and Die, Jefferson,

North Carolina: McFarland & Company, Inc., Publishers, 1996.

Gall, William. "A Military Perspective on Mount Belvedere." in Imbrie, John and Evans, Hugh M., ed. Good Times and Bad Times, a History of C Company, 85th Mountain Infantry Regiment, Tenth Mountain Division. Queechee, Vermont: Heritage Press, 1995.

Govan, Captain Thomas P. The Army Ground Forces Training for Mountain and Winter Warfare, Study No. 23, Historical Section – Army Ground Forces, 1946. Harper, Frank. Military Ski Manual: A Handbook for Ski and Mountain Troops. Harrisburg, Pennsylvania. The Military Service Publishing Company, 1943

Imbrie, John and Brooks, Thomas R. 10th Mountain Division Campaign in Italy 1945. Forest Hills, New York: National Association of the 10th Mountain Division, 2002. Imbrie, John and Evans, Hugh M., ed. Good Times and Bad Times, a History of C Company, 85th Mountain Infantry Regiment, Tenth Mountain Division. Queechee, Vermont: Heritage Press, 1995.

Imbrie, John. A Chronology of the 10th Mountain Division in World War II. Waterton, New York: National Association of the 10th

Mountain Division. 2000.

Jenkins, McKay. The Last Ridge

Lunday, Philip A. and Charles M. Hampton, The Tramway Builders: A Brief History of Company D, 126th Engineer Mountain Battalion, published by the authors, 1994.

Pote, Winston. Mountain Troops. 10th Mountain Division, Camp Hale, Colorado. Camden, Maine: Down East Books, 1982.

Reynolds, Whitman M. Medical Problems of Mountain Troops, Greenwich, Connecticut, 1942, 10th Mountain Division Records, TMD1, 10th Mountain Division Collection, The Denver Public Library

Sanders, Charles. The Boys of Winter. Boulder, Colorado: University Press of Colorado, 2005.

Shelton, Peter. Climb to Conquer, the Untold Story of WWII's Ski Troops. New York: Scribner, 2003.

Smith, Charles Page. "Reflections on C Company" in Imbrie, John and Evans, Hugh M., ed. Good Times and Bad Times, a History of C Company, 85th Mountain Infantry Regiment, Tenth Mountain Division. Queechee, Vermont: Heritage Press, 1995.

Thruelsen, Richard. "The 10th Caught it All at Once," in Saturday Evening Post, December 8,

1945

Whitlock, Flint and Bob Bishop. Soldiers on Skis: A Pictorial Memoir of the 10th Mountain Division. Boulder, Colorado: The Paladin Press, 1992.

Woodruff, John B. A Short History of the 85th Mountain Infantry Regiment. United States Army. November 1945.

Woody, Robert Letters of Memory in John Imbrie and Hugh Evans, Good Times and Bad Times, a History of C Company, 85th Mountain Infantry Regiment, Tenth Mountain Division. Queechee, Vermont: Heritage Press, 1995.

Manuscripts and Unpublished Works

10th Mountain Division Audio-Visual Collection, TMD204, 10th Mountain Division Collection, The Denver Public Library.

10th Mountain Division Newspaper Collection, TMD93, 10th Mountain Division Collection, The Denver Public Library.

10th Mountain Division Records, TMD1, 10th Mountain Division Collection, The Denver Public Library.

99th Battalion Papers, WH597, Western History Collection, The Denver Public Library

Dan L. Kennerly Papers, M2011, Western

History Collection, The Denver Public Library.
George P. Hays Papers, TMD61, 10th
Mountain Division Collection, The Denver
Public Library.
Irving Hale Papers, WH908, Western History
Collection, The Denver Public Library J.
Hunter Carroll Papers, M1996, Western
History Collection, The Denver Public Library
John D. Magrath Papers, TMD65, 10th
Mountain Division Collection, The Denver
Public Library
Norman Lindhjem Papers, TMD101, 10th
Mountain Division Collection, The Denver
Public Library.
Oliver James Barr Papers, TMD34, 10th
Mountain Division Collection, The Denver
Public Library.
National Association of the 10th Mountain
Division Records, TMD40, 10th Mountain
Division Collection, The Denver Public Library
Richard C. Johnson Papers, M1913, Western
History Collection, The Denver Public Library
Richard Wilson Papers, TMD30, 10th Mountain
Division Collection, The Denver Public Library.

Appendix

85th Regiment - Company K (TMD-188), unit
photograph June 5, 1944.

Left to Right TOP (forth) ROW, 1, Pietsch, John, 2, Newton, Spencer, 3, Elliott, Robert, 4, Fairfield, Eugene, 5, Brusse, Martin, 6, Samuelson, Milo, 7, Turck, James, 8, Easley, Maynard, 9, Teague, Everette, 10, Stokes, John, 11, Walters, Arthur, 12, Neufeld, Stanley, 13, Westran, Roy, 14, Clark, Walter, 15, Yost, James, 16, Pedersen, Oswald, 17, Kuhn, Heiko, 18, Pickel, Edwin, 19, Schuck, William , 20, Johnson, Ralph, 21, Scales, Nelson, 22, Homans, Elmer, 23, Monahan, Thomas, 24, Redle, Edward, 25, Brady, John, 26, Janovick, Steve, 27, Jacobsen, Sigurd, 28, Fandel, Joseph, 29, Englebert, Nicholas, 30, Conrad, Robert, 31, White, Leroy ?, 32, Langer, Ralph, 33, Hamilton, Martin, 34, Dreyfous, Paul, 35, Bendt, William, 36, Laurie, John, 37, Lewis, Edward, 38, Knott, Russell, 39, Power, William (Tom), 40, Todd, Donald.

Left to Right SECOND ROW, 1, Feigum, Marvin, 2, Loverme, Louis, 3, Ulmer, Wilbur, 4, Klauk, Charles, 5, Eastlund, Ralph, 6, Pacheco, Joseph, 7, Pelton, Ellis, 8, Duenas, Lawrence, 9, Allen, Charles, 10, Birkenstein,

Henry, 11, Clark, Merrill, 12, Gehringer, Robert, 13, Leveille, Francis, 14, Casoria, Carlo, 15, Braunstiener, Eric ?, 16, Bojczak, Henry, 17, Kiebler, Arthur, 18, Meindl, Theodore, 19, Leslie, William, 20, Johnson, Martin, 21, Schrader, John, 22, Moore, Robert, 23, Winkel, Robert, 24, McGowen, Patrick, 25, Smith, Gordon, 26, Thompson, Hans, 27, Yank, Robert, 28, Pinkston, Marvin, 29, Atwood, William, 30, Kovach, Benjamin, 31, Gifford, Sheldon, 32, Cavoli, Eugene ?, 33, Hampton, Howard, , ,

Left to Right THIRD ROW, 1, Harman, Willard, 2, Polek, Walter, 3, Polfus, Clarence, 4, Grzeda, Walter, 5, Rockenbach, Donald, 6, Ausevich, Edward, 7, Gonsoir, Fred ?, 8, McMahon, Carroll, 9, Ehrgott, Norman, 10, Bair, Eugene, 11, Newhall, Roger, 12, Clancy, John, 13, Galloway, Lawrence, 14, Popkin, Jack, 15, Larsen, Hans ?, 16, Barnes, Harold, 17, Toler, Art, 18, Stovall, Frank, 19, Bush, Benjamin, 20, Fox, Everett, 21, Drennen, Emerson E., 22, Edwards, William, 23, Clarke, Thomas, 24, Rivard, Jack, 25, Askwith, Harold, 26, Makela, Ray, 27, Piano, Victor, 28, Hitt, Clark, 29, Wakefield, Bruce, 30, Buhrmaster, Fred, 31, Tomasino, Alfred , 32,

Roddick, Robert, 33, Gadwood, Frances ?, 34, Pane, Frank,

Left to Right FRONT (first) ROW, 1, Kasper, Herman K. , 2, Winter, Frederick M., 3, Glaze, Ralph F., 4, Wolf, William, 5, Ellison, Herbert A., 6, Coscia, Oronzio , 7, Adams, Edward, 8, Byers, Ivan, 9, Raivo, Lester, 10, Schneider, Howard, 11, Wuerslin, Manfred, 12, Soeder, Louis, 13, Price, Frederick, 14, Hauptman, Charles, 15, Eggleston, Kenneth, 16, Collings, William, 17, Reiss, Thomas, 18, McCarthy, William, 19, Feldman, Daniel, 20, Charrette, John, 21, Schimke, Reuben, 22, Weil, Felix, 23, DeNoma, John, 24, Young, Stanton,

It is certainly ironic and little did I know that the cover photograph taken thirty years earlier, Circa 1982, at Pere' Antoine Alley behind the St. Louis Cathedral in New Orleans, Louisiana would play such a significant part in the end of my journey. My father lived only two miles away from Pere' Antoine Alley. There is no doubt in my mind that my father walked the same alley. It is probable we walked it together hand in hand.

Acknowledgments

First and foremost I want to praise the R. L. Polk City Directory.

My editor, Mr. Baker deserves his own medal for the miracle he was able to accomplish in the extreme editing of my book. Thank you John. (bakerltd@mail2world.com)

And, I am also grateful the 10th Mountain Division is still an active group.

Many thanks to Felicity Hallanan's editing and her hard work on the "Blizzard" newsletter published by and for the soldiers of the 10th Mountain Division. (admin@10thmdf.org) Subscriptions available.

In addition, I owe everything to my friend Bubby. He was the first and only person to validate my need to honor my father.

Special thanks to John Hagood and Jay Schmidt, my dream team, for the happiest day of my life in court.

Judge Landrieu deserves a special thanks; she held the power to mentally change my life.

This book could not exist if it were not for the diligence and hard work of the following people and institutions: at the 10th Mountain Division Resource Center, Mr. Dennis Hagen, present archivist; Ms. D. Gemar, past archivist; and Mr. Val Rios, past President of the Descendant's Association. I am extremely grateful for the special privilege extended to me by Ms. Coi Drummond-Gehrig of the Denver Public Library's Digital Image Sales and Research Department for use of their copyright photo of my father's unit, 85th Regiment, Co. K.

Thank you.

Additional Acknowledgments

Thanks to Mrs. Stevens, Michael S., Joann, Rick in Phoenix, Jim K., a few friends and, of course, God who helped me endure ten years of grief and ten more years of tears.

Also, - thanks to the characters in my life. I'm so happy I've had the opportunity to connect with each and every one of you. And even more thanks to the ones that are no longer with us.

All but a couple of characters' names were changed to provide anonymity. My intentions were never to disrespect anyone, but it's my truth.

Conclusion

Most people say they wouldn't change anything about their life. I would change everything. How could I be enchanted with getting to know my Father from his grave?

I'm learning with baby steps to deal with the fact that I missed the greatest part of my childhood and the opportunity to get to know the other half of me, my Father. I'm healing one day at a time. I am hoping that this book will reach someone who knows something about who my father really was, where he was really born, and what happened to his parents (my grandparents) who supposedly lived in Nanticoke, Pennsylvania from 1903 to 1920.

If you enjoyed this book, could you please return to Amazon and write a review. Your true comments would be greatly beneficial and appreciated.

Thanks to the people that purchased my book.

Author Contact Information

For comments and/or information please contact me at:

theukraineinme@gmail.com

www.ingramcontent.com/pod-product-compliance
Lightning Source LLC
Chambersburg PA
CBHW061142040426
42445CB00013B/1510